Table of Contents

Pronunciation

Chileans speak the Latin American version of Spanish (Castellano) that differs from that spoken in Spain in several ways.

Ñ = ('nyuh')

LL = ('yuh' or in some regions 'J')

A = (as in 'apple', never as in 'ape' or 'day')

Dedicated to my wife Amanda for her love and care. To Lillian Gonzalez and to Alejandra Manquilef for making it all possible.

Also, to those who welcomed and entertained me with hospitality and friendship; Mari Luz, Nelson, the Manquilef family, Paivie, Mette and all the others who I hold so very dear but unfortunately didn't fit in with the book's final cut.

And of course, to all the people of Chile

Prologue

The sudden scream took me completely by surprise, jolting me violently alert from my reverie. It had up until that point been a tranquil Friday evening and I had been staring idly out of the window. I watched as the distant orange ball of setting sun sank lazily towards the horizon. Its waning rays lanced horizontally out to me through the dust and heat of the dimming evening sky. They skimmed rooftops, grazed their way past large and elegant water towers, and filtered through the leaves of spring-time trees, before twinkling gently as they collided with the window pane's glass. Passing through it, the rays settled on the attentive faces of my students, who looked up at me from their classroom in the university at the end of the world.

I have found that true excitement usually strikes when it is least expected, and it was that tranquil evening late in an Araucanian Spring, that events were to take an unexpectedly sudden, and forbidding turn.

Up until that point my day had been unremarkable in almost every way. It was five-thirty in the evening and I was at my second job of the day; teaching an intermediate English course at the aptly named University of the Frontier (UFRO), down in the southern Chilean city of Temuco.

The students spread out before me all had one thing in common. All belonged to a little-known race indigenous to that part of South America; they were proud descendants of Mapuche Indians. They could be justified in their pride because, unlike many other native peoples around the globe, their ancestry had struggled for centuries through warfare, oppression, poverty and disease. Against Inca, conquistador and state oppressor they had fought, and in their struggles had withstood all who tried to subjugate them, bowed but never beaten.

Their oppression and suffering continue to this day, and there remain many who hold deep prejudices against them, some extremists even regarding them as a

7

lesser species. But unlike many other races now consigned to history books, special reservations, or hidden from sight in remote regions, the Mapuche and their precious culture live on.

A foreigner could be forgiven for mistaking a Mapuche for a native of central Asia, with their black hair and skin tone that is darker than that of the average Chilean of Spanish descent. The Mapuche that remain to this day live predominantly in the southern region of Chile named after the hardy Monkey-Puzzle Tree, a tree well known for its sturdy branches with exceptionally tough, spiky leaves.

These still grow widely on the slopes of the foothills and volcanoes in the mountainous east of the country and are known locally as Araucarias, the land they inhabit being the Araucania; Chile's southerly 9th region.

I had been in Chile for some time and had grown immensely fond of these people who were some of the kindest, warmest and most hospitable that I'd ever met. However, life for the previous couple of weeks had, for the first time, become a little routine. I was starting to miss the raw sense of adventure that I'd felt during my first few months in the country. It was tough going juggling four different jobs, which were spread right across the bustling city of Temuco.

Nevertheless, I was grateful for the increased job stability, and the money which was finally starting to trickle through. So it was in quite a relaxed atmosphere that I chatted away to my students that evening, teaching, listening, watching the sun go down and sharing the occasional joke.

It was during one such conversation that we were suddenly interrupted by a loud and piercing scream.

The scream was emitted with such ferocity that it seemed totally out of place on a peaceful weekday evening. It was not a screech of pain, rather one of anger, of battle. As I looked out of my first-floor classroom window, I was able to immediately locate its source.

Several 'protesters' of the type I had not seen for several weeks, were inside the university and charging out towards the main gates barely twenty metres from my classroom window. Armed with rocks, sticks and burning tyres, the scarves wrapped around their heads to conceal their identities bestowed on them an intimidating appearance, making them resemble the stereotypical image of a fanatical terrorist.

The gates were fashioned from thick, heavy steel and coated with dull blue paint. They were fronted with bars that began at the ground and continued right to the very top. I had barely time to register what was happening when these gates were flung aside as if they were made of paper, making a resounding boom as two large armoured police riot trucks smashed them open from the outside.

These trucks were covered with a thick green skin of fortified steel, fitted with powerful engines and rooftop water cannons. They looked squat, authoritative and tough. Their rather battered condition was a testimony to the frequent street battles that occurred in that part of Temuco.

They were known locally as 'guanacos', which is also the name of a small dear-like animal of the Llama family native to Chile. Among other things, this breed of animal is well known for its habit of aggressively spitting on anyone who strays too close. The police Guanacos that had entered the university that day then demonstrated that they too had a potent spit, as they traded powerful water blasts with the protesters' rocks, in the battle which was taking place just outside of my classroom window.

At that stage of my time in Chile this sort of incident was nothing particularly new to me. I had already been very close to similar scenes of civil unrest on numerous occasions, and had experienced a broad range of emotions on my various adventures.

Previously I'd walked through lines of rock-throwing protesters, had Molotov cocktails exploding mere metres away and had been tear-gassed half a dozen times. I was also almost stranded in the world's driest desert, buried by the Chilean Army for a night under the snow, and had only narrowly escaped being savaged by a raging farmyard cow with nothing but her life to lose.

However, for some reason this time I felt a little different. A real sense of nervousness washed over me, and I found it very difficult to concentrate on what it was that I was supposed to be doing. I took a quick couple of photos out of the classroom window, then tried to ignore what was going on outside to concentrate on my teaching. But it wasn't easy. My hand began to shake, and my voice wavered slightly. It must have been obvious to my students that my mind was elsewhere.

On most of the previous occurrences I had felt more excited than fearful, the perception of danger could even have been regarded as enjoyable at the time. But on those occasions, I had been participating in such activities of my own choice, having weighed up and accepted the risks beforehand.

Whether heading out at night to try and take pictures of the rioting, or deciding to climb a volcano when every other party that day had turned back, I had usually made sure that I knew what I was getting into, calculating and accepting each risk in advance.

This time I was in no real danger, but the suddenness and confusion of it all coupled with the fact that I was responsible for all my students was daunting. Was this just the prelude to the carabiñero special forces storming the building and dragging off the students as they had done in the past? Or would the protesters seek refuge from the waves of teargas inside my language building? The immediate future was a total and intimidating unknown to me.

Fortunately, the carabiñeros eventually withdrew. They were forbidden from entering the university grounds without special permission, and the sounds of battle then moved to a different part of the campus. In no time at all the class was over and I was hurrying downstairs ready for the mad dash across the city to my third job of the day.

On the way out our kindly secretary, Yessica, warned me of the dangers outside and told me to try and find an exit that wasn't blocked by the troubles. I thanked her and made my way out across the lawn, which just fifteen minutes earlier had been the scene of the dramatic disturbances, but for the time being was clear.

A quick glance to my left revealed the all too familiar scene of burning tyres and hooded figures blocking the roadway. The smell of burning rubber filled the air, and the acrid smoke from the tyres was thick enough to make visibility difficult. On this occasion I did not have time to investigate more closely, so I made my way out of the side gate, though the back streets and down to the bus-stop. I hoped that I'd somehow beat the chaotic downtown traffic and make it to my next job on time.

A Turbulent Paradise

It was 1999 when John McCarthy and Brian Keenan published a book about their travels along the length of the distant land of the country of Chile. Their names mean little to most people now, but between 1986 and 1991 they were held hostage by Islamic Jihad Terrorists in the middle eastern' state of Lebanon, where they achieved the undesired feat of being Britain's longest held hostages in that terrible conflict. Throughout their long incarceration in a horrific Lebanese prison cell, they had little with which to occupy their time but dream of what things they could achieve, if they were ever to regain their freedom.

One of these dreams was to travel the length of the South American country of Chile, and appreciate some of the many wonders which existed outside of their small, isolated and dingy cell. They hoped to see if their idealistic imaginings of that far-off land would bear any resemblance to the reality.

The reason that I draw attention to this here is that they chose to entitle the book of their travels; 'Between Extremes'. This is by far the best description that I have found to encompass the varied geography, people and culture of that faraway, long and slender land.

Chile is known for being the thinnest country in the world. Barely a couple of hundred kilometres in breadth at its widest point, yet it boasts territory stretching from equatorial Peru to the frozen depths of Antarctica. It encompasses almost every different type of terrain and climate extreme that our planet has to offer. The north of the country; a vast area known as the Atacama Desert, is the driest area of land in the world. It is a place where in some parts there has never been any recorded rainfall. Heading further south takes you through the region surrounding the city of La Serena, not only world famous for the quality of its wine, but also for producing the country's national drink; a fierce grape-based concoction that goes by the name of Pisco.

Continuing downwards brings you to the vast urban sprawl of the capital city Santiago. It is located in the central valley and is almost surrounded by the awe-inspiring Andes Mountains, which form the backbone to the entire continent. It is where the vast majority of the country's population lives, and the only international point of entry by air. However, whilst nightlife, shopping and history are amongst many facets of interest to a visitor or tourist, like many major cities it has its fair share of problems. With overcrowding by traffic and buildings, contamination by crime and pollution, it often feels suffocated in the summer by a claustrophobic heat. It is a place that whilst having much to commend it, is not somewhere to linger if natural beauty is what you desire.

Heading further south still, you pass through the large regional capital of Conception and then onto the city of Los Angeles; the last urban centre before entering Chile's 9th region. Also known as the region of the Araucania, it is a place of incredible natural splendour. Home to the native Araucanians, or Mapuche as they are known, it has attracted prospective conquerors for hundreds of years. First from the Incas of the North,

16

then the Spanish conquistadors with their superior military might and technology, right up until the arrival of the Chilean state itself.

Despite having the odds consistently stacked heavily against them, the Mapuche people have resisted all attempts at subjugation and, despite a severe reduction in numbers and lands, continue to survive. The peace treaty of 1881 between the Mapuches and the young Chilean state was signed on Ñielol Hill in the regional capital city of Temuco, bringing a peace that has held ever since. But despite the wars being over, life for the natives of this fertile land was not destined to be easy, and their problems continue to this day. I was able to gain an insight into the intricacies and complexities of life in this region, as it was to be Temuco where I would be spending much of my time in Chile.

To the south of Temuco lies the beautiful and wet city of Valdivia, with its elegant parks, flowing rivers and resident sea lions. Continue for several hours further down the Pan-American; Chile's main north-south artery, and you arrive at the city of Puerto Montt.

Puerto Montt is a large port city famous for its seafood and for being the gateway to the turbulent

17

iceberg teeming seas to the south. Between here and the southerly city of Punta Arenas lies a landscape that has been tamed by neither man nor beast. So inhospitable is this land of glaciers, mountains, impenetrable forests and raging seas, that it has to this day never been possible to construct a road to pass through it. Therefore, to travel south from Puerto Montt it is necessary to take a ferry for 4-5 days through the fiords, islands and icebergs, before disembarking at the port of Punta Arenas.

Anyone stepping off a ship into this port at the end of the world will be entering a city that although isolated, has an adventurous history spanning its short existence to rival any other. To the south of Punta Arenas lies a hostile land across the Magellan Straight called the Tierra del Fuego; Land of Fire. I remain unsure as to how it was awarded such a name, as the driving rain, fierce wind and freezing cold climate are to me the antipathy of everything that resembles heat and fire. Perhaps the brave discoverers of this far off land did indeed possess a sense of irony.

From the dry, burning deserts in the north, the freezing, snow-shrouded vistas of the far south, the crashing violent waves of the Pacific Ocean on the west coast, to the treacherous high slopes of the Andes to the east; it is clear why Chile is a country of geographic extremes. Perhaps it is this geography that has influenced the demographic makeup of the country. It is not just the physical factors of this land that can be considered extreme, but also the social and political ones.

Although it is not as large as in many other South American nations, there still exists in Chile a great divide between those who are rich and those who are poor, the haves and the have-nots. It can be difficult for the casual observer to notice such a divide, but after several months in Temuco it really began to strike me how the middle and upper classes live comfortably in their fortified houses in the suburbs. Surrounded by high metal railings they travel in their new pick-up trucks and 4x4s, whilst just a 20-minute walk down the road brings you to an area where people scrape a bare existence on the streets, in communities that are little more than shanty towns.

All of this must of course not be taken out of context, the poor of Chile are still considerably better off than those of other countries in Latin America and indeed many of those in the wider world, with a government that tries harder than most in its attempts to assist them. This still doesn't lessen the impact of seeing a man on the street outside a prosperous department store, not begging for money, but for milk without lactose to keep his baby alive for just another few days.

It seems impossible in the west to get an appreciation of what poverty truly is without viewing it first-hand. Chile has no state funded social welfare or an equivalent of the National Health Service. Therefore, a person suffering through illness or accident with no money to pay for treatment, must either continue to bear their pain or seek other 'alternative' methods of therapy.

The people of Chile seem to be as divided politically as they are financially and socially. In recent history Chile has gone from being ruled by a socialist government under a democratically elected Marxist president, to seventeen years of military rule under a right-wing dictator, (or military governor, depending on your affiliation), under whose government all other political parties were banned. From 1990 to 2010 the country was led by a leftist coalition government who although socialist by name, were very much aware of the need to tread very carefully to avoid returning to the violence and upheavals of the past. In 2006 Chile passed a significant milestone electing the first ever female president of the Latin American continent; Michelle Bachelet. 2010 saw the election of the first successful right wing presidential candidate since the dictatorship; a charismatic multimillionaire businessman called Sebastian Piñera.

Therefore, when conversing with a Chilean with whom one has no prior acquaintance, caution is advised as there is no easy way to tell one man from another with regards to where their allegiances may lie. In the west we often have the luxury of being able to judge issues according to simplistic black and white, right and wrong criteria. The Socialist Allende government aimed to share the land far more evenly between the rich and poor, eliminate economic inequality, and end the foreign exploitation and dominance of Chilean industries.

Few could argue with these admirable intentions, nor could a reasonable person dispute the fact that General Augusto Pinochet seized power in a violent military coup d'état (which had substantial tacit support from the United States), proceeded to eliminate many of his political opponents, and ruled over a regime infamous for its killings, disappearances and almost total lack of freedom of expression or democracy. This is a simple factual description of a turbulent time in Chile's past, and it is the one almost universally represented in the international media. Unfortunately, real life is far from black and white. The simple goodies and baddies that we are so comfortable to believe in, can take on an uncomfortable complexity when placed under the harsh spotlight of reality.

Indian Country

Temuco. It is a name that still brings a smile to my lips and a slight ache of fondness to my heart.

The capital of the Araucanian region of Chile; it is the centre point of the Mapuche heartlands, and was my home for the ten months that I spent working and exploring there. It sits in the southern part of the country below the drier wine growing regions to the North, but above the hostile and rugged terrains on the way down to Tierra del Fuego.

Temuco is a city that embodies the theme of extremes and contrasts which run throughout all strata of Chile's society and geography. It lies on a plain that is ensconced between the vast peaks of the Andes range

23

to the East, and the wooded hills of the 'Coastal Cordillera' with the Pacific Ocean beyond to the West.

I gazed out at these impressive views through the window of the jet aircraft as it descended towards Temuco's tiny airport. Beneath it the waters of the wide and shallow Cautin river flowed down from the Andes and hugged the city's Eastern edge. It was these waters that the plane followed, as it floated downwards towards the short runway.

Landings at Temuco have always had for me a slightly hairy feeling; all that you can see below you as the aircraft gets increasingly lower are the turbulent waters of the Cautin. The plane descended lower and lower, but just as it seemed that impact with the river was inevitable, the runway suddenly appeared beneath the wheels and we touched down. Powerful G-forces kicked in as the aircraft braked sharply to stop before the end of the short landing strip.

Stepping out into the baking heat of the Chilean summer, sweat already began to pour from my forehead as I collected my bags, then headed through the airport and out onto the street beyond.

Looking around past the taxi drivers and policemen, my heart leapt as I spotted the smiling excited face of my dear friend Alejandra Manquilef, as she ran towards me and with a shout of mono! Despite being greeted by the Spanish word for monkey, I was delighted to see her, and she soon wrapped her arms around me with the passionate embrace of a dearly missed friend.

I threw my bags into the back of her weathered red pick-up truck, and jumped inside as she tipped the parking attendant and we began our short journey into town. My emotions were a tumult of delight at being reunited with my friend on her home turf, and fascination at the sights and sounds of the totally foreign environment that I now found myself a part of.

My eyes grew as wide as saucers as I tried to drink in the detail of this city that seemed so different to everything that I knew. Houses that appeared ramshackle and dilapidated shared streets with modern apartments, oxen pulling carts vied for space on the road with modern SUVs, and packs of stray dogs mingled with both beggars, and shoppers at high end department stores.

It didn't take us long to pass through the city centre and get out into the suburbs. The age and variety of the buildings and houses fascinated me as we drove along 'German Avenue' past large and ornate wooden houses that could have been plucked straight from the American mid-west more than a century ago. Weaving between brightly coloured local buses we passed three different universities, one of which looked like a cross between a grand country mansion and a witch's tower, and another an impressively grand white building fronted with large marble columns in the style of a Greek temple.

I felt so happy to be in this place, the hometown of my most cherished friend on the other side of the earth to all that I knew. I had met Ale barely two years earlier; I was in my final year of studies at Coventry University and was looking for someone to rent a room in our student house. I still remember standing on the doorstep with a guy called Pete on a bright summer's day, as we wondered what kind of outcast, freak or loser would want to share a house with a pair of oddballs like us.

We were very pleasantly surprised when instead of the expected spotty student weirdo, we were met by a bright and gorgeous Latin American girl with kind eyes and a dazzling smile and looks that were matched only by her intellect.

For exact reasons which still elude me Ale agreed to stay. Our friendship grew closer and closer, until a couple of years later I found myself on an aeroplane with a one-way ticket to Chile, for no other reason that I couldn't think of anything else better to do.

My sightseeing came to a temporary halt when Ale slowed the pick-up and pulled into the drive of her parents' bungalow; the house of the Manquilefs.

Manquilef is an unusual surname even in Chile and points to her family's Mapuche heritage. Her parents made a slightly unusual couple, and it was thanks to their early care and boundless hospitality that I was able to really feel at home in those first difficult weeks of life in a foreign land. Her mother; Edith Bächler, was one of the many Chileans in the region originally of German descent. With her blonde hair and pale skin, she appeared more western than Chilean, earning her the nickname 'Gringa' among friends. She was evidently the town beauty in her youth.

The lucky man who she chose to marry was Oscar Manquilef, a professor of physical education at UFRO who had a history of mountaineering, and owned a farm out of town which was passed down to him through many generations of his Mapuche ancestors. It was to this farm that we would be heading for the weekend.

But before the trip to the farm, Ale had already made plans for what would be my first few days in the land known as 'The Araucania'. She decided that I should see the Pacific Ocean for the first time and visit a small town on the East Coast; a place called Puerto Saavedra.

For the morning of my impending Saavedra trip I had been relaxing in Ale's house, and feeling rather reluctant to head out into the unknown and scary world beyond its four walls. Ale was having none of it though. She was determined to help me to discover Chile in the same way that a mother bird helps her new-born young to discover if they can fly; by manner of unceremoniously throwing them from the nest into the wild and unfamiliar world beyond the confines of its cosseting walls.

After reeling off a highly detailed, unpronounceable and impossible to memorise set of instructions, Ale sent me out the door for my first experience travelling solo in a foreign country.

With barely five words of Spanish in my vocabulary, I managed to flag down one of the 'Collectivo' shared taxis which follow set routes through Temuco's bustling streets, before pulling open the door and climbing in. I wedged myself inside between a suited businessman and a plump mother and her child.

Via some very poorly-pronounced pigeon Spanish, I attempted to explain to the driver the street name of my desired destination. I then sat back and tried to enjoy the experience of travelling, despite a growing feeling of trepidation in my chest.

One by one the other passengers left the Collectivo as we passed through Temuco's prosperous commercial centre with its modern shopping areas, and the shining office tower of Torre Campánario.

Coming out the other side of the contemporary middle part of the city, the quality of the streets and buildings began to decrease dramatically. Potholes and road works blighted every avenue, litter became more apparent, and packs of large stray dogs weaved their way between cars and people alike.

Eventually the driver pulled over at the side of a road that was impassable to traffic, and indicated that this was to be my stop. Pointing through the throng of people, market stalls and dogs, he reeled off a list of directions that I could neither understand or comprehend, and bid me goodbye.

Feeling very vulnerable as I made way through the road works and along the packed streets, my head was ringing with the various warnings I had received from Edith Bächler, and Ale, about how dangerous the streets of Temuco were.

I couldn't have stood out any more even if I'd painted myself green and stripped naked; I was certainly the only gangling westerner nervously shouldering an oversized army surplus backpack on the streets of downtown Temuco that day.

Almost immediately I became lost, and began to wander the streets in search of the elusive bus station. Half an hour of this fruitless wandering left me tired and demoralised, so I sat down on a bench in one of the city's public squares to gather my thoughts, regain my composure and plan a course of action.

I had barely begun to get my breath back when two women approached. One was middle aged and looked as though she'd had a hard life; haggard in appearance but with sharp and piercing green eyes. The other who I presumed to be her daughter was much younger, in her early teens with a more innocent look about her and a youthful complexion. Both women were unusually dressed in long, flowery patterned but dirty gowns, and carrying small handbags full of trinkets by their sides.

At this point I remembered something that Edith had said to me the day before:

"Beware the Jedanos Tom, they will catch you unawares, take advantage of you and steal from you".

Jedanos is the Chilean slang word for Gypsies, and at the time Edith's warning had sounded rather strangely specific to me. I wasn't aware of any Gypsies in Chile and certainly couldn't understand how they would pose any more of a threat to me than anyone else.

I had taken it to be another miscommunication issue or perhaps some mild racism or prejudice, and quickly forgot that our conversation had ever occurred. However now that the two Jedanos were in front of me, the elder already with her hand outstretched for money, Edith's warning began to ring in my ears.

"No" I said with as much authority as I could muster. Undeterred, the older woman still held out her hand and began to babble out words that were incomprehensible to me.

"No" I said again, shaking my head and waving my hand as I tried to persuade the two women to give up and go away.

The babbling continued and outstretched arm remained unmoving, and I realised that there would be no dissuading them, so I grabbed my pack and got up to leave.

"Por favour, por mi bebe" said the young girl suddenly. At the same time she pulled up the top half of her gown and exposed her swollen belly.

This caused me to pause. The girl didn't appear to be a day over 14, so to already be pregnant and spending her days begging on the streets of Temuco meant that the future could not have been bright for her.

"Mi bebe?" she said again, looking up at me with puppy dog eyes.

I relented, pulled out my wallet and opened it, intending to give her some money before continuing with my journey.

I was not to get away so easily however. As soon my wallet appeared it was as if I'd unveiled a big bag of freshly ground crack at an A-list celebrity party. I tried to get out a solitary note to hand to the girl, but both Jedanos simultaneously lunged forwards and before I could react were rifling through all the money that I had in my possession to get me through the following few days' worth of travelling.

"No! No! Oi! Give it back!" I shouted and tried to snatch the wallet back.

But it was to be to no avail as I was pushed away by both surprisingly strong women, whilst they tried to reassure me with a chorus of *"no no no, es ok, es ok"*.

After removing all my notes, they handed my wallet back and held up the money up in front of me. Ignoring my continuing protestations, the older woman managed to get me to sit down and pulled forward my hand, so that it faced palm upwards in front of her. She then delved into her handbag and removed a plastic bottle of water, and a small but greasy looking leg bone that looked like it may have come from somebody's chicken dinner.

As the Jedanos had not yet run off with the money, I naively held out some hope that I may yet have it returned. Barely speaking a single word of Spanish, I could not bring myself to shout for help from the police or one of the locals. I would not have been able to explain the nature of my problem and, as bizarre as it sounds now, was nervous of appearing foolish.

Spitting on the chicken bone, the woman continued to babble away as she rubbed the disgusting object all over my hand as part of some kind of weird ritual. Next, she moved on to the money.

Opening her bottle of water, she began to pour it all over the cash, soaking it as best as she could and adding in a gob of her spit for good measure. She then proceeded to roll the notes around in her hands, squashing them smaller and smaller, adding more spit and water as they began to steadily disintegrate.

I grew even more frustrated as the money fell apart before my eyes, my feeble protests met by further forced reassurances from both the woman and girl. I still naively hoped that this was all just some cruel magic trick from which the cash would somehow emerge intact at the end.

Rubbing her hands together the woman smiled and indicated that the ritual was now over, but instead of revealing the money intact, perhaps from behind my ear in the manner of a children's magician, the pair simply turned and walked off, soon disappearing into the crowds.

Trying to get over what had just happened, I felt very alone sitting helpless at that moment in that foreign city. Depressed that I had just lost all my travelling money, I was also very ashamed that I had just been robbed in broad daylight by a woman and a girl, without even putting up any effective resistance.

My obvious next course of action would have been to return to Ale's home. But despite the hilarity that this would undoubtedly bring to her and her family, I couldn't face the shame of failing so spectacularly on my first trip out of the house. I resolved to continue to

Puerto Saavedra despite my losses, still nervous but also more determined than ever to succeed.

Luckily, although the Jedanos had seen my emergency travellers' cheque they had not understood its purpose, so I had managed to keep hold of it. After having it exchanged at a dishevelled looking money outlet, resplendent as it was with bullet marks in its windows. I then made my way through the city to the rural bus depot, and with the help of some friendly locals managed to board a hardy looking microbus.

For the next few hours the bus rattled its way through the fields and up and down the hills of the western Araucanian countryside. Whilst less rugged than the east of the country, the western slice of Chile between the central plains and the sea is nevertheless very beautiful. It is still a very rural place, with villages, farms, forests, fields and many settlements which remain owned and populated by the native Mapuche people.

There are also still visible impressive remains of the development which occurred in the late 19th and early 20th centuries. Old abandoned railway tracks weave their way along overgrown trails, connecting towns which still display gently rusting steam engines at their entrances. Intricate iron bridges, which are the equal of any Victorian British engineering, span raging white rivers which slow and widen as they get nearer to the sea.

Squeezing along narrow country lanes, past heavily loaded logging trucks, buses and farm vehicles, the bus shook and bounced its way nearer to the coast whilst the surrounding terrain gradually became smoother and gentler, as steep hills made way for coastal plains.

By now I was one of the bus's few remaining passengers, so when the doors banged open and the driver shouted 'Puerto Saavedra!" I dismounted and began to take in my new surroundings.

Around me I could see that Puerto Saavedra was flat and low lying and made up of the type of wooden bungalow houses which are typical across the smaller towns of Chile. The town itself seemed rather deprived and was unremarkable apart from its pleasant seaside location.

It was this very seaside location that had played a major role in influencing the area's recent history, for in the year 1960 Chile was hit by the most powerful earthquake in recorded human history. It was a 9.5 magnitude monster which devastated the south of the country and brought in its wake a massive tsunami which washed away many coastal towns and villages.

The disaster was so grand in scale that it reshaped much of the geography of southern Chile, deepening rivers, burying buildings and creating huge new areas of wetlands. Puerto Saavedra was right in the tsunami's path and took the full brunt of its impact, resulting in thousands of deaths amongst its ill prepared populace.

The deaths didn't quite end at Saavedra with the tsunami's receding waters though. As this gruesome tale illustrates what can happen when poorly educated people with strong superstitions collide with powerful forces of nature:

"In the coastal village Collileufu, Lafkenches (Mapuche people who live and identify with the coast and sea) carried out a ritual human sacrifice during the days following the main earthquake. Collileufu, located in the Budi Lake area, south of Puerto Saavedra, was by 1960 highly isolated and inhabitants there spoke mainly Mapudungun.

The community had gathered in Cerro La Mesa, while the lowlands were struck by successive tsunamis. Juana Namuncura Añen, a local machi (a type of shaman), demanded the sacrifice of the grandson of Juan Painecur, a neighbour, in order to calm the earth and the ocean. The victim, 5-year-old José Luis Painecur, had his arms and legs removed by Juan Pañán and Juan José Painecur (the victim's grandfather), and was stuck into the sand of the beach like a stake.

The waters of the Pacific Ocean then carried the body out to sea. The sacrifice came to be known after a boy in the commune of Nueva Imperial denounced to local leaders the theft of two horses that were allegedly eaten during the sacrifice ritual. The two men were charged with the crime of murder and confessed, but later recanted. They were released after two years. A judge ruled that those involved had "acted without free will, driven by an irresistible natural force of ancestral tradition."[1]

Well I hoped that my journey in these Mapuche coastal lands would involve neither tsunami nor human sacrifice. Especially as being a slender bespectacled gringo, I would possibly make a rather better beach stake than an innocent five-year-old boy!

39

I walked up and down the streets of the little town but could not see anything particularly remarkable about the area. I began to wonder why Ale had picked this location for my first foray into the Araucanian interior.

I made my way along a dusty and rutted track towards the beach, and before long mud turned to sand and for the first time in my life I cast my eyes on the slowly shifting waters of the Eastern Pacific Ocean. A sudden sense of peace crept over me, as I felt the trials and tribulations of my journey so far begin to melt away into the quiet stillness of the surrounding air.

I noticed that rather than having an unrestricted view of the open sea, I was in fact on the eastern shore of a large bay which had been carved out of the sand by the twin forces of the ocean current and the wide waters of the river Imperial.

Determined to see the Pacific in all its glory, I continued round the bay until I had made my way to its western edge. I was now standing on a tree covered sandbar which projected out into the ocean like a finger, shielding the interior from the powerful forces beyond its reach.

Treading carefully I worked my way through the trees, climbing around and over their many intertwined stumps before they thinned out and revealed a clear view of the unfettered Pacific which now lay before me. I had been warned by Ale and Edith before I set off not to swim in the ocean at all costs. I had not taken them seriously at the time, as I had arrogantly believed that as a strong swimmer I could handle a bit of a splash about in the waves.

But I now saw for myself the reasoning behind their concern. I could see the power and force behind the waves which built up suddenly from nothing and smashed themselves into the land where beach met water. Ale and Edith had told me that many people die in Chile each year by underestimating the strength of waves, being knocked over and sucked out to the depths before even being aware of what has hit them.

Standing in this place I felt that I had gone beyond the edge of my known world. In my life and education up to that point I had accumulated awareness of far off places around the globe, having garnered some knowledge of their peoples, geographies and histories.

But Chile I had barely heard of before meeting Ale, so this shoreline which was remote even by Chilean standards felt isolated, and this isolation brought with it a deep sense of peace. No-one back in the UK in my 'real' life, would ever be able to find me where I now was. In turn no-one in this place knew of me, of what I had done, what my weaknesses were or what my failures had been.

The Pacific waters which stretched out beyond the far horizon, then onwards for many thousands of miles until the next habitable land, felt like an un-crossable barrier. They formed a kind of shield from the concerns of the wider world.

My fears and anxieties slipped away like crisp brown leaves off an autumnal tree, and I began to feel like a truly free man. I now understood why Ale sent me to this place.

Feeling enriched and filled with a sense of satisfied peace, I felt the temperature begin to drop and the winds pick up as the day drew to an end. I turned, collected my pack and began to trek back around the bay to the relative civilisation of Saavedra town.

As I began the walk up the beach with the sea to my back, three figures appeared over the crest of a dune in front of me. They drew closer and I saw that they were young men in their late teens, dressed in loose work jeans and faded t-shirts.

As soon as they spotted me they began to point and chat excitedly amongst themselves, seemingly none of them had seen a westerner before. I began to get anxious as they drew closer and closer, the warnings from Ale and Edith about danger being around every corner bouncing around my head as I became only too aware of how isolated I was.

There was no easy way of avoiding them, so before long I stood face to face with the three lads. They broke the silence first with a babble of Spanish phrases, and I replied in the only way that I was able:

"No entiendo"

Upon hearing this declaration of non-understanding, they stared for a few moments before babbling at me in Spanish again, a little slower this time.

43

"No entiendo" I repeated, wondering for how long this charade would continue.

Confounded, the men muttered between themselves before one pointed to his chest and declared *"Chile!"*, then pointed to mine and raised his eyebrows in a quizzical manner.

"Ah" I finally understood, pointed to myself and declared *"Inglaterra"*. A wave of excitement seemed to spread throughout the group on hearing this, because as one they hit me with an eager stream of Spanish. To my ears it sounded like:

"Saohgoiuragskbglkearutasfd?"
"Sorry I don't understand"
"Rengsohfsongyotter?"
"Nope, sorry don't know what you're talking about"
"Engeadnakjonyotten?"

I shook my head, resigned to the fact that my first intercultural exchange between myself and the people of Chile was doomed to failure due to the insurmountable communication barriers.

I prepared myself to bid them farewell before attempting to make an escape, when something in their last question clicked into place in my head.

"Hang on a minute; Johnny Rotten?"

"Si, si, si!" they exclaimed, dancing around on the spot with joy at the success of finally getting through to the particularly dense gringo in their midst.

I stood there puzzled and utterly bemused at the fact that in this remote corner of the world, the single most relevant thing about the United Kingdom to a group of local people, who didn't possess a word of English between them, would be a 70s Punk singer called Johnny Rotten!

The more that I listened to them talk, the more that my ears seemed to tune in slightly, and whilst I understood the meanings of few words or phrases, I slowly began to communicate. With the word 'Anarchistas' the trio explained that they considered themselves to be anarchists, which explained their love for Johnny Rotten. They also explained they were ethnic Mapuches, to which I responded with an enthusiastic cheer.

Despite hardly any words of each other's languages, we somehow managed to converse and even laugh along together on that isolated beach at the end of the world. Eventually though the evening drew in, and we bid each other farewell before going our separate ways.

Back in the town of Saavedra, I located a place by the side of the road which was marked out with the sign of a tent. Calling it a campsite would be a far too optimistic description, as it was little more than a collection of garden sheds presided over by a gap-toothed man in a dubiously stained vest.

Nevertheless, for the price of £6 it was adequate for my needs. I paid the proprietor his due and settled down for the night on top of a large square of packing foam which served to function as a makeshift bed.

After a reasonable night's sleep I departed for Temuco the following morning, catching the bus for the long trip along the rural roads back into town. On arriving back at the Manquilefs' house I declared my trip a success, and regaled them with stories of the adventure which had seen me taking my first baby steps into the real Chile outside of my comfort zone.

I was not to rest for long. The following day we packed a huge amount of food, drink and various belongings into the Manquilefs' two off-road vehicles and headed out of town. Weaving our way through Temuco's suburbs, we soon crossed the River Cautin alongside the expansive and towering ironwork of an old rail bridge. Its flaking red paint was a testament to the engineering achievements of the frontiersmen of generations past.

I visited this 'abandoned' bridge subsequently on one of my many explorational forays around Temuco, and had enjoyed the thrill of trying to cross it on foot. As I jumped from sleeper to sleeper I could see the fast moving and frothy waters of the Cautin far below, distant enough to make death a certainty should any fall occur. Nevertheless, I was enjoying this fooling around like a child in the bright afternoon sunlight. At least I was until I looked up and saw the steel face of a large train at the other end of the bridge, coming straight towards me.

Panicking I looked around but there seemed to be nowhere on the bridge to hide. It was too far to go back, there was an oncoming train to my front, and a 50 foot drop down to the boulder strewn river below. My only option was the road bridge which lay parallel alongside the rail crossing, but they weren't directly connected, and there was a gap of over a metre between the two.

Seeing my obvious distress, an elderly local man who was short in stature with kindly eyes and a plastic bag on his arm, stopped midway through his crossing of the road bridge. Turning towards me, he leant forwards over the guardrail and reached out, beckoning with a word in Spanish which I assumed to mean "Jump!!".

I took in a deep breath, stole a final glance at the puffing and groaning beast of the train oncoming to my left, and jumped.

My feet landed on a ridge jutting out from the base of the other bridge, and I grabbed hold of the guardrail for all I was worth as the elderly gent grasped my forearm. Moments later the train passed behind me, rumbling and shaking its way towards its destination in central Temuco. Climbing over the rail, I steadied myself and tried to regain my breath whilst my rescuer laughed to himself at the randomness of the strange situation.

Back in the Manquilefs' car we finished crossing the bridge and joined the Panamericana. Turning south we travelled for some time until reaching the small rural town of Quepe. Here we pulled off the highway onto a gravel track, which wound its way between fields and around horses, oxen and hitchhikers before arriving at the entrance to the isolated farmstead.

I was glad to have arrived finally at the farm. It was such a secluded and tranquil place that not in a million years would anyone be able to find me there should I not wish them to. On this occasion there were quite a few of us who were visiting. Ale's brother Peque was there with his English girlfriend and two of his friends from Santiago. Then there was Ale, her parents and an elderly Aunt. There was also a small group of local men, who worked as part time farm-hands when they weren't tending to their own cattle and lands.

One of these men was short in stature but displayed a constant happy demeanour and a welcoming smile. He introduced himself to me as *'Pistola'*. When I enquired as to the meaning behind this unusual name he showed me his hand; which was missing the ends of several fingers because of an accident in years past. It

49

made Pistola look like he was permanently holding his hand in the shape of a pistol. He was married to a kindly woman called Meche; short for Mercedes, and they lived together in a small wooden house with a vegetable garden behind the farm's main barn.

It was good to see Ale's brother again. I hadn't seen him since a year earlier, when he had come to the UK, and had lived in our house in Coventry for a short time whilst he tried to learn English. Although his real name was Oscar; after his father, he was known to all by the ironic nickname of Peque; Tiny.

There wasn't much that was tiny about Peque. At six-foot-tall and broad to go with it he was bigger than average for a Chilean. But it was his self-confidence and force of personality that really made him seem larger than life.

When I had first met Peque I had been in my final year of studies at university. I was sharing a house with Ale, who brought many friends and acquaintances from Chile and across South America to our home on a regular basis. Before long I was unwittingly thrown into the social side of Latino culture, as we hosted many parties and dinner nights with groups of Chileans, Peruvians, Columbians and Spaniards amongst others.

Although I didn't know it at the time, I guess that the experience acted as kind of a warm-up for my future plunge into the deep-end of living in a Latin country.

Peque had arrived during this period and soon made himself at home, despite an almost total lack of ability to speak or understand the English language.

Now whereas you or I might have all sorts of different priorities of vocabulary to learn when immersing ourselves in a new language, they are likely to follow a standard theme. Phrases such as; *please, thank you, I want, I like, where is, that, this, him, her, how much, how far and I don't understand* are all useful words that will help a person to survive their first few days in a foreign land.

This wasn't for Peque though. Peque was a Latino man's man, half Mapuche but 100% Chilean. For him there was only one word that he desired to know the English equivalent for; the word *weon*.

Weon is a word seemingly unique to Chile. About the only accurately definable statement that it is possible to make about it, is that *weon* is a Chilean slang word and usually an expletive.

Apart from that, it seems that the various applications of the word *weon* are as infinite as the orator's imagination. It can be a verb, an adjective, a noun or a pronoun. It can be intended as a term of offense, a term of endearment, a simple description of what you are doing or just a word put in at random to stretch out a sentence.

It can mean; mate, dude, him, her, them, fucker, shit, buddy, pal, stuff, things, person, object, animal, arsehole, cretin, great guy, stupid guy, or lazy person. However, in its verb form, *'weando'* it means; messing around, wasting time, taking the mickey, fooling about, winding up, joking, passing the time, taking the piss or simply just doing something, but it can also mean doing nothing.

A common discourse amongst two Chileans in anything but the most formal and polite of situations will usually go something like this:

"Hola weon, como estai po weon?" Hi dickhead how are you doing mate?

"Bien weon haciendo puro wea no ma po weon." I'm good dude, do nothing but pissing around mate.

"Wena weon, solomente weando no ma entonces. Que es esta wea?" That's good mate, just messing around then. What is this shit?

"Es mi auto po weon, dañado por mi hermano weon catchai?" It is my car mate, damaged by my brother mate, you get it?

"Que weon po weon, esa weon no se puede hacer esa tipo de wea weon!" What an arsehole mate, that fucker cannot do that kind of shit mate!

And so it goes on, and on and on. Despite being the recipient of one to one tuition in the finer points of swearing and slang, from dozens of Chilean men and women during my time in Chile, I was never to truly get the hang of the word *weon*. I generally knew what people meant when they said it, but I always feared using it myself. This was for the simple reason that I could never really be sure, whether I was referring to someone as a mate or calling him a total arsehole!

Peque however decided that the intricacies of the English language were unnecessarily complex, when all he wanted to do was find a simple single alternative for his favourite Chilean word. After some consultation with his elder sister Ale, he decided on a word that he would go on to use liberally, interspersed with his other English vocabulary with scant regard for grammar or context forever after.

Unfortunately, the word that he picked was wanker.

It took a while, but I eventually got used to being greeted by the term; *"hello wanker!"* shouted out with great confidence and volume whenever I bumped into Peque in the street or in our home. However, as you might imagine, this did cause problems in certain social situations.

Our shared house in Coventry was on the edge of one of the city's poorest and most dangerous estates at the time. We didn't suffer any real trouble when we lived there, but we had to be alert and streetwise when travelling alone, taking care not to accidentally stray down the wrong street at the wrong time.

On one occasion I was walking back from uni, when coming towards me along the footpath I spied a sort of half man, half ape type character, who wore jeans, a black bomber jacket and an angry scowl across his face. His sunken pig eyes stared at me from inside his shaven skull as he marched towards, me taking up as much of the foot-path as possible with his body's ample girth.

My spider senses started to tingle in anticipation of a threat, so I prepared to cross the street in a pre-emptive effort to avoid any confrontation. But then it happened:

"Hellooooo Wanker!!!!" came the familiar greeting, shouted from the doorway of my house across the street at significant volume.

Stood in front of the house was Peque, dressed in nothing but a pair of aging blue underpants and grinning from ear to ear at the sight of his English amigo.

Ape-man turned, a look of confused rage spread across his face as he sized up his semi naked abuser. As the Ape man seemingly pondered who to punch first, I did the only thing that I could think of to save our skins. I shouted:

"Hello Peque wanker! Yes, it's me, the wanker! Hello I'm the wanker! I'm your wanker!"

As I voiced this bizarre tirade I kept clear eye contact with Peque, and began to walk towards him trying to make it as clear as possible that I had been the intended target of the Chilean's offensive greeting.

It seemed to work. Ape-man's fighting stance changed to one of hesitant bafflement, and he seemed to decide that it wouldn't be worth the effort to tangle with these very strange two men, who were evidently afflicted with some kind of weird mental illness. So, keeping an eye on us from across the street he ambled along on his way, perhaps seeking out more normal human company.

On the farm in Chile Peque greeted me as normal; *"hello wanker"* and introduced his incredibly well-spoken and polite English girlfriend called Sarah. The two had met in a bar in Birmingham, where Peque had been working as a glass collector to fund his English lessons.

Once the chaos and fluster of arriving and unloading the vehicles had subsided, Ale told me that her father, Oscar Senior, was going to kill one of his cows to provide meat for a great feast and party. This would be a rare and special event indeed and as a foreigner, and until recently a stranger, I was to be privileged to witness it.

I had neglected to bring suitable boots for the wet and muddy countryside conditions so, to the amusement of the Chileans, I wrapped my feet in some plastic carrier bags and made my way towards Oscar's barn. Leaving the grounds of the main farmhouse and its carefully tended garden, smartly pruned bushes and tidily clipped grass, I ducked into a tunnel formed through some densely growing undergrowth, and felt my way along through the wet vegetation and tall leafy cane plants. They surrounded me on all sides and came together above my head, blocking out all but a few weakly glimmering rays of distant ochre-tinted sunlight.

The trail though this verdant world was narrow and hemmed in by plants on every side. Half-way through, it crossed a small area of wetland, where balancing along thin logs which were attached to trees several feet off the ground, was the only way to progress.

Emerging once again into the light, it was if I had transited through a passage between worlds. I had left the civility and orderly beauty of the farmhouse behind and was now in the working part of the farm.

To my left lay a pen full of plump pigs that snorted and snored as they fidgeted and shuffled around, and beyond them was a wooden fenced enclosure full of young horses. Grassy fields surrounded an old barn full of gently rusting equipment and a veteran tractor that remained in use, despite having seen many decades of prior service. The whole scene reminded me of the American Midwest in miniature, and it seemed a perfect retreat from the pressures of the city.

Oscar, Peque, Pistola and a tall wiry but tough looking Mapuche called Pelao, who had an aura of a hard frontiersman about him and wore a long knife in a leather scabbard by his side, were waiting for me inside the barn. There were no women present; they had all remained back in the farmhouse, chatting and preparing food for the weekend's feasting. Next to the barn was a small field of cattle in which stood the cow which was destined to be dinner for the next few months, at this point oblivious to her imminent change in fortune.

I was quite excited at the prospect of seeing an animal killed for the first time, not for any morbid reason, but because meat is something that many us take for granted. I had not harboured any real moral qualms about eating meat, but I had thought that if one is to be an omnivore, then one should be prepared to kill, butcher and cook an animal, and not to kid oneself that all meat is born into plastic packaging inside the icy confines of a supermarket's refrigerator.

The animal was not particularly big by cow standards, but there was still enough meat on her to feed a family very well for several months. Standing calmly in a narrow wooden enclosure, her brown fur almost blended in with the woodwork around her. It was not long before Pelao had tied a rope around her small horns, and we all then helped to haul her into the nearby barn.

By now realising that something was up, she began to resist and weighing as much as a cow does, she managed to put up quite a fight. It took the strength of all the men present, myself included, to gradually reel her in closer and closer to the barn's sturdy central pillar.

After she was roped in tight to the base of the pillar, Pelao unsheathed his very large butchers' knife from the scabbard attached to his thick leather tool belt. It had a long, keen blade and a sharp point, making it ideally suited to the task to which it was about to be put. Distracted by the small crowd of men in front of her, and restrained by the taught rope, the nervous beast showed no sign of realising what fate was about to befall her.

With a sharp downward jab, Pelao stabbed the knife downwards down into the back of the cow's neck, intending to sever the spinal nerve and therefore save the animal from any unnecessary further suffering by paralysing her before the fatal blow was delivered.

It immediately became apparent though that something was going wrong. Instead of collapsing to the ground and awaiting her fate, the cow reared up with such force that the rope holding her down jerked taught and then parted with a loud snap! Suddenly instead of being in control of our situation, we were at the mercy of an angry powerful animal, quite capable of doing us serious damage with a determined charge.

As she turned on me the cow pointed her horns, which before looked small and unthreatening, but now seemed like the lethal points of half a ton of desperate beast, as they took aim at my chest. My body tensed up as my panicked mind tried to decide whether to fight or take flight, when neither option seemed likely to see me escape unharmed.

Fortunately, help was on hand in the form of Pelao who, with all the mastery of an expert frontiersman, tied the end of a nearby rope into a quick lasso and hurled it through the air. The open loop of the lasso landed perfectly on target around the cow's stubby horns, to be snapped tight with a quick tug.

The situation now calmed down, the cow could be paralysed properly, and the final act delivered. As she sat facing us on the barn's dusty floor, Pelao plunged his long knife deep into her chest, and her eyes began to fade as life ebbed away. In the minute or so that it took her to die, I was surprised to discover that I felt no particular emotion at what was happening.

Things then took a further turn for the surreal. The cow's throat was slit, and a large bowl placed underneath to collect the blood that gushed forth in a thick deluge, to accompany the already full tub of dark, deeply scarlet blood beneath her chest.

It wasn't long before Oscar motioned for me to come over to him. He had with him the two large plastic containers, both now brimming with the cow's fresh blood and small floating chucks of meat and gristle from inside of her throat.

Wondering what was going on, I was further confused when Oscar motioned for me to drink.

"I'm sorry what?" was my surprised reaction, sure that I'd either missed something in translation, or was the subject of some kind of macho Chilean joke.

He continued to indicate that he wanted me to drink as I eyed the thick red liquid in front of me. Liquid that only moments before had coursed powerfully through the cow's veins. By now I realised that I had an audience as I glanced around to see all the men stood watching me, Mapuche eyes looking seriously from expectant faces.

As I saw their eager stares, I realised that what was happening was no joke. In fact it was more of a test, a test that I would have to pass if I were ever to gain their respect. With much trepidation I leant forward as Oscar raised the container to my lips, giving me a close-up view of the thick crimson blood that was sloshing back and forth, tinged only by the green speckle of a diced herb that had been sprinkled on top.

I took a gulp, then another, the blood still warm as I swallowed it. I anticipated that I would gag and spew up the unnatural beverage, but to my surprise the taste was nowhere near as bad as that for which my trepidations had prepared me. The bitter herbs took the edge off the flavour, and the warmth made it more palatable. After my third gulp Oscar bade me to stop and passed me a glass of red wine.

"Drink Tom, drink" he said as I took repeated sips from the glass, in the process washing out the taste in my mouth and calming my churning stomach.

I looked up, seeing smiles and bright wide eyes on the faces of those around me. I then began to receive hearty pats on the back from the proud Mapuche, accompanied by comments of *"bien gringo, es un buen gringo"*. I realised then that I had passed my unexpected test and had been accepted into their midst.

I passed the remainder of the afternoon doing my best to help with the butchering; something that seemed to involve me trying to hold onto large slippery pieces of cow meat, whilst Oscar attacked them with a circular power saw.

I spent several hours nervously clenching my teeth, as he chipped away with the rapidly spinning blade within millimetres of my fingers. This was interspersed with brief moments of horror when the blade would catch unexpectedly on a bone, causing Oscar to shout

"Chuta!" and the whirring buzz-saw to veer terrifyingly towards me!

Once the preparation of the newly deceased cow was complete, the time came to join in with the Manquilefs and friends to celebrate with a traditional Chilean barbeque or 'asado'.

Chileans seem to take at least as much pride in their barbeques as Australians do, and have elevated the outdoor cooking of meat into almost a cultural art form. Our asado took place around a dilapidated wooden shack that was used for the storage of farm tools, firewood and for hanging meat. Ten of us sat cosily on small log stools and benches in near darkness. Our faces were lit only by the warm and flickering light from the flames of the Asado, as they licked the base of a huge metal pan which was scorched and blackened from many previous celebrations.

The huge open pan was filled with delicious fresh meat, sizzling intensely in a sauce rich in onions, herbs, oil and litres upon litres of wine. It was a barbecue the like of which I'd never seen. It was a pleasure merely to dip a piece of bread into the meaty sauce and suck out the rich oily meat-juices within.

I felt like a highly honoured guest. Everyone present regaled me with gifts, food, plentiful drink and generally treated me like visiting royalty. At the same time I seemed to be an endless source of amusement for all present, my every action and expression the subject of curiosity and humour.

Although I had managed to overcome the great challenge of swallowing mouthfuls of warm cow blood, there was still more to come, in the form of a large soup made from all the most unappetising internal pieces of the recently deceased bovine.

Known as cocemiento, the thing was disgusting, but once again I was egged on by all around who urged me to persevere with this new challenge. I was quickly learning the importance of appearing 'manly' in the extraordinarily macho culture which is prevalent amongst Latino men, from the tip of South America up to Mexico and all the lands in-between.

I poked around my deep bowl of dark brown meaty juices, sipping the fatty liquid which tasted pleasant enough by itself. But each probe only served to disturb what lay below, greeting me with the sight of platted white chunks of intestine, veiny lumps of viscera and other assorted guts as they rose and fell, bobbing briefly to the surface before sinking once again down to the bottom of the bowl.

Whilst doing my utmost to disguise my revulsion, I chewed and choked down as much of the 'soup' as I was able. Helping it down with as much alcohol as I could manage, it was with an immense sense of relief that I eventually reached the bare surface of the bowl's bottom.

"You like Tom? You like?" asked one of the revellers as he displayed a huge grin.

Despite it having been blatantly obvious to all around what a struggle it had been for me to consume the meal, I gave a typically English response to avoid causing any offense and replied that it was *"very nice"*. However, I could not hide the awkwardly strained look which was spread across my face.

"He loves it!!!" Shouted one of the Mapuche and all around cheered in jubilation.

"Really Tom? You like?" asked Mercedes as she stared at me with a look of disbelief spread across her face.

"Err, oh yes, very nice" I repeated, continuing with the lie that was convincing no-one.

"More! He wants more!" the shout went out as everyone cheered and laughed.

At this point I had to concede defeat and drop my facade. Shaking my head and saying *"no, please god no"* I pushed the bowl away, unable to face a second helping.

By now though it seemed that I had properly earned my spurs and was treated with great warmth and mutual respect by all around.

The evening continued with much drinking, deliciously cooked and ample food, laughs, music, karaoke and dancing, before the night drew to an end and in ones and twos people made their way to bed.

I walked out alone and lay on my back in a nearby field. Relaxing my body and mind, I stared up at the millions of crisp stars and clouds of faint nebulae which stretched out across the sky in the wide band of the Milky Way Galaxy.

As I lay there I pondered the twin wonders of the warmth of the local people, who treated me more like a brother than a stranger, and the wondrous interstellar marvels above, which I had never seen the like of before.

As I saw more and more of Chile I would come to learn that the warmth and hospitality of the people was almost as ubiquitous as the stars which lingered thousands of light years away in the sky above.

***

Despite my adoration of Chile's geography and culture, I was not in the country as a tourist and would need to work to survive. Prior to my departure from the UK I had managed to do some preparation for this. Ale had arranged for to meet her friend and mentor, a lady called Lillian Gonzalez, who came to stay for a week in the freezing cold house which I was renting at the time out in one of the suburbs of Coventry.

Lillian had looked rather out of place in our small and cramped house which had no central heating or shower. In which I slept on a deflated airbed on the floor surrounded by junk, because I couldn't afford a mattress. At the time I was a thin and pale former student, holding down a soul-destroying job entering data for a logistics company.

These were not the best of times, but thanks to the friendship and humour of my two dear friends; Alejandra Manquilef, and an intensely witty and intelligent Mancunian called Paul, I was able to stay sane. I lived a minimalist existence, squirreling away a few pounds each week in the hope of turning my dream of a trip to Chile into a reality.

Lillian on the other hand carried herself with a regal sophistication. Well dressed and professional, she was a kindly and adventurous soul who was visiting England as part of her career as an esteemed teacher of English, and international fellowship ambassador.

At that time nothing could have been further from my mind, than the idea of teaching English, or teaching anything in fact. The idea of standing up in front of a class of teenage students absolutely terrified me. I much preferred the idea of working in a more solitary career, something technical perhaps with minimal potential for confrontation.

I guided Lillian around the sights of Coventry such as they were; Lady Godiva who sat naked on top of her horse in the town centre, the expansive motor museum, and the bombed-out ruins of the old cathedral where in the deafening silence, you can still feel the presence of the thousands of souls obliterated by German bombs, in that terrible war only a few generations ago.

I felt slightly humble in Lillian's presence; she was an incredibly talented woman of the world who had achieved great things in her field, and could count her friends in the hundreds. Whereas I had nothing to my name but a degree in a field I wasn't even sure that I still wanted to work in.

Nevertheless, Lillian seemed to be courteously content with my amateur attempts at hospitality. Smiling even as I showed her what remained of Coventry's damp medieval backstreets, she was delighted by the simple pleasure of a pint of ale in one of the city's 400-year-old pubs.

During this time she must have seen some hidden potential in me, as the conversation came around to the possibility of me teaching English in Chile. The more we talked, the more that this seemingly ridiculous idea took root inside my mind.

After a couple more months of saving pennies and losing my sanity at the logistics firm, I completed a crash course in teaching English, packed a few changes of clothes into an old Army surplus back-pack, and boarded a one-way flight around the globe to the distant land of Chile.

For every ounce of hospitality that I had given Lillian in the UK, in Chile she repaid me a thousand-fold. Her tastefully decorated house lay on a pleasant side street on the outskirts of Temuco, and became my base for the first few months of my stay. Her husband Claudio seemed to be on a personal crusade to ensure that I was slightly inebriated for every hour of the day. He was ever on hand with glasses of beer, high quality wine and intoxicating Pisco, none of which were offers that I was ever able to refuse.

Lillian had pulled some strings and managed to get me a job teaching English at one of Temuco's universities; the aptly named University of the Frontier. However, there was a twist. I would not be teaching a regular class of mixed students, I was to be working as part of a project called RÜPÜ.

RÜPÜ is a word from the native Mapuche language of Mapudungun and means road or pathway. The RÜPÜ project is an initiative to encourage Mapuche students who have suffered repression under Pinochet or prejudice from some parts of Chilean society, who are at an educational disadvantage due to their largely poor and rural backgrounds.

71

Teaching English as a foreign language may seem a rather strange way to encourage a native people to better value themselves and their heritage. Nevertheless the project combined workshops in Mapuche history, culture and language with more traditional subjects, and it seemed to deliver positive results.

I was supposed to have already started teaching three weeks beforehand, but the city of Temuco had been in the midst of a fierce bout of student unrest when I had arrived. Many of the city's universities were in a state of siege. Huge piles of tables and chairs blocked the entrances, whilst groups of students manned the barricades day and night, warming themselves around improvised oil drum braziers.

Lillian told me that these sorts of protests were quite frequent, and that a short time ago the police had gone into UFRO with 'tanks' to clear out the students. She said that sometimes the protestors would set fire to the whole street in front of the university, and that there would be a high chance of protest tomorrow.

As if the prospect of teaching in a foreign country where I barely spoke the language wasn't intimidating enough, I now could add riots and turmoil to the list of things I would have to deal with. At the end of that day I wrote in my diary simply:

"I'm going to have to work harder, and be braver, than ever in my life."

The next day we drove to UFRO for my first proper sight of the university. The air of tension aside, it was a pleasant-looking and open campus with characterful buildings of various shapes and sizes, emerald green grass all around and many flowers. Colourful political murals were painted on the walls, many depicting the 'evil' government oppressing the students, whilst others were in memorial to young people killed rebelling against Pinochet.

Our entry to the RÜPÜ project part of the campus was blocked by a barricade of about 15 students. Approaching them I felt very nervous, but tried not to show it. Teachers were not particularly welcome at that time, and as an obvious foreigner I stood out far more than most.

Fortunately Lillian managed to negotiate our way past, after promising that we wouldn't be teaching or working. Hidden right at the back of the campus was our destination; the small thatched huts of Proyecto

RÜPÜ. The huts, known as rucas, were replicas of the traditional Mapuche homes still found in parts of the countryside today. With oval bases and walls often made of densely packed wood and mud. They have pretty peaked roofs of thick interwoven grass, and are cosy and warm inside.

After being introduced to the friendly and smiling staff and meeting some of the students, we left and made our way once again past the barricades, thanking the protestors as we passed by.

The next day I went in by myself to sit in on one of the English lessons. The campus seemed peaceful, but when I arrived at the languages building the doors were locked, and blinds had been pulled down over all the windows.

Luis; one of the building's caretakers, saw me waiting and emerged from the gloom inside to let me in. There was a subdued atmosphere within. A few students sat in front of computer terminals in the dark studying in secret, and no teachers were to be found. The tension in the air was tangible, and I wondered if was justified. Surely we wouldn't be attacked simply for studying?

Lillian arrived and with an anxious look on her face told me that the protesters were serious, that we mustn't be caught studying as it was dangerous. She made it clear that we must leave immediately. We hurried outside to her car and drove off, only to find our escape route blocked by rock-toting balaclava clad militants.

Pulling a 180° turn we joined a small group of other cars heading for the university's side entrance, but that too was blocked by a group of intimidating youths, who also hid their faces behind balaclavas and scarves.

We followed the vehicle in front's lead, and gingerly wove our way between the 'protestors' and managed to make it through unscathed. I had never seen Lillian as serious and concerned as she was on that journey home.

Her expression fell into an even deeper look of worry, when an ambulance screamed by with lights flashing in the other direction, heading towards the university grounds.

The following day saw the university beset by further battles and yet again I was unable to teach a class. By now my course was over three weeks late starting, and the protests showed few signs of abating. Despite the battles I managed to make it inside the university again in the hope of finding something to do, but it was in vain as the danger meant that no classes were being held.

Luis and Alvaro; the language building's two caretakers, seemed to feel a duty of care towards me, and they would go on to look out for me during my entire time at UFRO. On this occasion they tentatively escorted me outside during a calm in the storm. Earlier I had caught glimpses of protestors battling police past the university's fence, but now Luis and Alvaro scanned the surroundings with eyes and ears to see if it was safe for me to leave.

"Es peligro?" I asked them in pigeon Spanish if it was dangerous.

After a brief silence Luis replied *"No.... es tranquillo"* confirming that peace had descended for the time being. Thanking them I left, making my way past the remains of burnt tyres, broken bottles and the coconut sized rocks which lay scattered in the street outside.

It would be another two weeks before I would be able to start teaching my first class. I busied myself in the meantime by learning as much Spanish as I was able, looking for other teaching work and exploring my new surroundings.

By this point I desperately needed a haircut. After traipsing around the city for days without seeing a single barber's shop, I managed to find a well-hidden shopping mall that had four floors full of them.

Why am I bothering to mention such a trivial thing you ask? Well describing what type of haircut you desire in a foreign country, where no-one speaks English, and you have barely 50 words of the local vocabulary to your name, is not an easy task.

Entering one of the stores I sat down in a padded chair. The barber asked me a question in Spanish. *"Corto"* I shouted, unsure whether I had said 'cut' or 'short'. The man then pointed at the back of my head and muttered something unintelligible. I replied *"Si"* to which he nodded in approval and began to hack away.

20 minutes later I walked out, relieved to find that I didn't look like an escapee from a mental institution, but instead sported a reasonably smart looking Chilean buzz-cut.

The protests and riots had done me a favour in a way; they had allowed me time to begin to establish myself in Temuco without too much pressure from work. However gradually they began to subside and in the last week of May D-Day arrived; the day that I would begin taking classes of up to 30 university students by myself.

Arriving at the university for my first full day of teaching I was nervous and hesitant. The watch on my wrist ticked steadily on its unerring course to signal the time to the start of my first lesson. As the minute hand got closer and closer to zero hour, my angst built up to almost unbearable levels. So instead of heading straight up to the classroom, I ran into a toilet cubicle downstairs and sat down. Stomach cramping, breathing racing and heartbeat pounding, I wanted to be sick, I wanted to cry, and I wanted to run.

What on earth was I doing! Here I was in South America with barely a few words of Spanish in my vocabulary, about to face a class of 30 university students and attempt to teach them my language. Surely I would be mocked, chastised and laughed at. I felt destined for failure, certain that I would embarrass myself, Lillian and all who knew about my journey to Chile and what I had set out to achieve.

Zero hour came. I could hear the hustle and bustle of students in the class above me and knew that I could delay my fate no longer.

Sliding back the latch on the cubicle door I stepped out into the corridor. But instead of running hell for leather for freedom, I found that my legs turned left, carrying me up the stairs, through the double doorway and into the classroom.

A sea of brown faces and black hair was there to greet me. A few wore friendly smiles, some expressions seemed harder, but most had a look of uncertain and nervous expectation. It seemed that they were every bit as unsure about me as I was about them.

Lillian came to the doorway, putting me slightly at ease with a warm smile and glint of humour in her eye. Welcoming me to the university, she introduced me to the class and announced that I had come all the way from England to teach them and to exchange cultures with them.

Bidding me good luck, Lillian soon departed and I turned to face the class.

One by one I introduced myself to the students in English as I had been instructed, and straight away I realised that I was dealing with a wide variety of ability within the group. One student, a young man called Luis, seemed to speak English almost as well as I did, having learned from his love of watching movies and talking with foreign visitors to his parents' guest house.

Others though did not understand a word, not even knowing the word 'hello'. Many of the girls especially seemed nervous at meeting an Englishman for the first time. Somehow I made it through the lesson in a slightly chaotic but overall not too disastrous a manner. Once the students had departed I allowed myself a sigh of immense relief. I had survived my first lesson, and I'd done it without being booed out of the room, abused, lynched or treated with any of the shocking disrespect that I'd occasionally shown my own teachers during school and university.

As the weeks went by I gradually grew more and more confident. I found that the young Mapuches were filled with a desire to learn. Each week my classes were full of their bemused but eager faces. They gave up their spare time to come and study, whilst expressing their curiosity about my background, upbringing and impressions of Chile and its people.

I probably learned more Spanish from them than they did English from me, but I think that we all benefitted in different ways. I had three different classes overall, and in time this grew to encompass other projects at UFRO, and lessons at other universities in Temuco.

In fact, after my first few months I was working not only at UFRO, but also the prestigious Universidad Catolica and Universidad Autonoma Del Sur, helping English Teachers at Collegio Montessori, teaching government workers at the environmental agency and giving private lessons to students, lawyers and a horny dentist.

I guess I'd better elaborate a little on the dentist.

His name was Eduardo. He was one of my private clients who could already speak English and wanted *'classes de conversation'* to improve on his fluency and vocabulary. I loved teaching classes de conversation because it generally wasn't very difficult, and sometimes all I had to do was talk to a person for an hour whilst

81

correcting the occasional word or point of grammar. It often felt like money for nothing.

Eduardo had his own dental surgery in an upmarket part of Temuco, close to a large and opulent shopping mall. Whenever I went there I would make myself known to one of the receptionists, who all seemed to be young and very pretty Chilean women, and then took a seat and waited for Eduardo to become available.

I could be waiting there anything between five and forty minutes as Eduardo finished drilling and filling whichever patient he had in at the time. But eventually he would emerge, strip off his apron and latex gloves, and sit me down for a chat.

Although he was middle-aged, Eduardo seemed youthful in both mind and body. Despite my initial attempts to remain professional, our conversations usually sank to the intellectual level of a couple of sex and booze mad teenage boys. No matter which bland subject I attempted to start the lesson with, he would rapidly lose interest and instead turn the conversation towards one of his favourite topics; drink or girls.

In our first lesson we covered in the space of an hour the topics of: beers from around the world, and different types and qualities of pisco within Chile. Eduardo seemed to delight in hearing about my experiences of Chile, and was especially keen to ensure that I would not leave the country before sampling the many alcoholic delights that it had to offer.

Soon the talk turned to women and Eduardo regaled me with tales of his favourite strip club adventures. It felt rather odd that I was there as an English teacher, dressed in smart shoes, spectacles and a shirt, holding a book of vocabulary under my arm, discussing the finer points of beer and strippers with one of Temuco's most elite professional dentists. He was paying the fees though, so who was I to argue?

I barely had to even do any actual teaching. Eduardo was already very fluent and seemed to be paying more for the company of a foreigner, than to actually be taught anything. However, I did try to help him a little. In the middle of a tale about one of his favourite nightclubs in the USA, he stumbled a little with his vocabulary and looked at me quizzically for an answer:

"There is an amazing club in the USA that is full of gorgeous girls with nice bodies. They all dance in skimpy

83

clothes it's such a great place. But the best thing is that the DJ has a really loud horn and when he blows it all the girls in the club,..... um they...um..."

"Dance?" I offered in response to Eduardo's puzzled look.

"No, they... umm.." he said as he searched for the right words inside his mind.

"Jump up?" I suggested.

"No, no they....."

"Shout out?" I tried, determined to be of some use in my professional capacity.

"They show their tits!!" Shouted Eduardo with glee. He seemed proud and delighted that he had dredged up this critical piece of English phraseology, which surely must be of so much use to someone in the dental trade.

After a while Eduardo mentioned that he had a niece and began to talk about her. At that point I naively thought that we had left the topics of sex and booze behind us, but I was soon to be proved wrong.

"Yes, she is a very nice girl. She works on the other side of town, in a discotech called 'Fire'".

With that he handed me a flyer for *'Fire'*, emblazoned as it was with the silhouettes of several lithe and bronze-bodied naked young women.

"The best thing is she has a friend, who is so beautiful I cannot believe it. Beautiful face, beautiful body, beautiful everything! Seriously, sometimes I think of her when I'm operating on patients, and whenever I do, my hand starts shaking around like this…"

And with that, Eduardo mimed holding onto a dental drill above a helpless patient's mouth, hand shaking away as if he had a sudden onset of Parkinson's syndrome! All the while with a look a sheer orgasmic glee spread across his face.

Despite the interesting variety of characters that I met during my various teaching jobs, UFRO remained where my heart truly lay. In time I came to love my students and many become close friends, inviting me into their homes and taking me on trips with their families.

My lessons however never became the epitome of teaching professionalism, and regularly descended into farce as I tried to explain concepts in ways that would be entertaining and intelligible.

Luis was a great help in the early days; often helping to translate between me and the other pupils whilst I refined the technicalities of his grammar and punctuation.

One day I was teaching the topic of food and boys and girls names to a class that included two of Luis' amigos; Bernado and Renato. Bernado was a slightly quiet but kindly young man who was a skilled guitarist, whereas Renato was more of a big friendly giant. Obsessed with talking about sex, he often shocked some of the female members of the class with his crude outbursts.

I liked them both but tried my best not to laugh along with Renato most of the time in the interests of upholding my thin veil of professionalism.

To teach the new vocabulary I was doing a role-play where I played a waiter, and the students had to describe various types of meal.

Me: *"And what would you like to eat sir?"*

Bernado *"Salmon"*

Me: *"Good choice. Would you to like to choose your salmon sir we have several,* (time to throw some English names into the mix) *he is John, he is Philip, he is Peter."* I

86

said as I pointed towards an imaginary restaurant fish tank.

Bernado: *"Hi do you have any women salmon?"*

This threw me slightly, why would anybody specifically want to eat a woman salmon?

Me: *"Err....yeah, err she's err Sarah.... and she's err... (women salmon?).... erm"*

Renato: *"Silvia Saint?"* the name of an American porn actress very popular with Chilean men.

Me: *"Erm.. No!"*

Renato: *"He knows! He knows!!!"*

Why anyone would want to pretend to eat a pornstar fish was beyond my comprehension, but sometimes the English classes just went that way.

It wasn't all just crudeness though, there were also moments of beauty. The following week Bernado and Renato brought in their guitars. The theme of the lesson was learning English through the songs of The Beatles and it was delightful to spend an hour singing along with my increasingly confident students. I explained the lyrics as I went to the accompaniment of Bernado and Renato strumming out magnificent melodies, that drifted out the open windows of the classroom and across the university campus.

I tried often to make use of media to give some variety to the classes. Upon telling another teacher that I had just shown my students footage of the first moon landing on the BBC, she suggested that I try comedy. She said that her students had enjoyed an episode of 'Friends' that she had shown them, although she had struggled to explain the significance of the phrase "teenie weenie".

I decided to try a similar approach, but to promote British interests I chose to show an episode of Blackadder starring Rowan Atkinson and Rick Mayall.

It probably wasn't a good choice for a basic English class; the actors spoke very rapidly, and used many colloquial phrases. Also, I hadn't bothered to check the episode myself before showing it to the students, and was slightly unprepared for all the vulgar language and sexual innuendo that it contained.

The students watched with foreheads furrowed deeply in confusion, as Rick Mayall acted out the role of a stupendously over the top WW1 pilot ace and irresistible sex object; Lord Flashheart.

I soon realised that the easy canned laughs of American humour were probably more appropriate for new learners of English. My students couldn't make much sense of Captain Blackadder's snide remarks, or of Flashheart thrusting his groin around the onscreen set.

The episode culminated with Flashheart coming face to face with 'The Red' Baron Von Ricthoven. The Baron makes a long and elaborate speech in the manner of a Hollywood arch-vilan explaining his evil plan, when suddenly and without warning, Flashheart pulls out a pistol and shoots him dead, declaring; *"What a poof!"*

This elicited the only response from my students throughout the entire programme. One of them looked at me and asked with a very confused look on his face:

"Que lo que es, poof?"

It was not a teaching technique that I repeated.

Another day another class, and a fresh set of Mapuche students sat before me. By this point my Spanish had improved significantly and I could now use it to explain many of the concepts of the English language that I had struggled with previously.

I became close friends with three of them; a guy called Ramon, his sister Mariana and their friend Yohanna. All three were from the pretty and rural town of Pitrufquen, located 30kms to the south of Temuco.

I first became acquainted with them during another role-play session. This time I was trying to teach a class on tourist vocab; airports, taxis, restaurants, hotels etc.

Ramon played the part of a tourist arriving at an airport and getting a taxi with three of the female students. Unfortunately, much of the vocabulary that Ramon knew seemed to be based around the various names for different alcoholic drinks. So, he decided to act as if he was on some sort of drinking holiday.

By the time we got to the restaurant part of the role-play everyone involved was acting drunk, even the girls drinking and staggering around pretending to order whiskey, vodka and wine as the other pupils in the class laughed and chipped in with whatever English they knew.

They seemed to delight in teaching me Spanish even more than I did in teaching them English. One of the most popular themes being:

'Things to shout at pretty women when you see them in the street'.

So, when, after some prompting, I shouted to the class in my poshest English accent:

"Quien es tu papi mijita rica!" (Something along the lines of 'Who is your daddy'), I had many of them doubled over with laughter, tears rolling down cheeks. The timid and disadvantaged Mapuche students that I had been told to expect on starting my work seemed to have come out of their shells.

***

September in Chile is an interesting month to say the least. It contains two dates that in the way they are remembered could not be more opposite to each other. The first is the 11th of September 1973; the year of the violent coup which resulted in seventeen years of military rule, and often brutal repression of the populace. The manifestation of this in modern Chile is that every year in the week leading up to the 11th of September, there are often a large amount of demonstrations and unrest, some of it violent, principally centred around the major cities.

Most of the news coverage of this is usually focused on Santiago, but due to its significant Mapuche population who were heavily repressed under Pinochet, Temuco also has more than its fair share of troubles.

The second key date falls merely seven days later, on the 18th of September; Chile's Independence Day. This is an annual celebration of the events that took place in 1810, when Chilean nationalists declared their autonomy from the Spanish colonial government which had been weakened by French occupation under Napoleon.

Full freedom would not be gained for another eight years however, when Chilean forces led by the national hero Bernardo O'Higgins, fought their way back from exile in the Andes mountains and consolidated the independent Chilean state.

It can be difficult for a foreigner (particularly a British one) to appreciate the significance of an Independence Day, but this is certainly not a problem that burdens the average Chilean. In modern day Chile the 18th is the conclusion to a solid week of eating, drinking, dancing, partying and patriotism.

It would easily be possible to write an entire book on Chile's culture and customs alone, but I'll summarise by saying that these things are strongly emphasised throughout the Independence Day celebrations. Alcoholic drinks are enjoyed to the full, including wine, whiskey, pisco and many more. A special part is played by a beverage known as chicha, a fermented drink that can be made from a variety of fruits and one that dates back to the time of the Incan Empire.

During the Incan period it was made from a type of maize by women who were taught the technique in special feminine schools called Acllahuasis. In these schools, women would learn Inca lore along with other useful skills such as spinning and weaving. The chicha of modern day Chile however is usually fermented from apples or grapes. It varies considerably in quality and strength, but is roughly equivalent to a weak cider.

Food plays an important part in Chilean culture, with many dishes tracing their routes to long before the country's founding and often being unique to particular regions. One snack that is enjoyed throughout the land though, (and on September the 18th especially) is the ubiquitous Empanada. Empanadas are basically a kind of stuffed pastry and come in two varieties; fritas (fried), or del horno (baked, literally 'from the oven'). They come in many different shapes and sizes and contain a wide range of different fillings.

The empanadas fritas were my personal favourites; stuffed either with hot melted cheese or a mixture of mince, onion and egg, they made a great if rather unhealthy snack. Whereas the baked empanadas were a meal in themselves with their larger size and much thicker pastry, they commonly had a meat or seafood filling complimented by onions and an olive.

After food and drink, the third ingredient for any successful September 18th celebration is without a doubt dance, especially the national dance which goes by the name of Cueca. Dance is an important part of life in every Latin country, particularly in Chile where Salsa, Meringue and Cumbia are among the more popular forms.

From an early age every school child is taught the national Cueca dance. Although like many things traditional its popularity is fading, it is still widely practised and must be danced by all as part of the Independence Day celebrations. I got my first inkling of its importance, in the same place where I learnt much of what I came to know about Chile, in my classroom.

It was in a lesson which was as normal as any of my classes ever were. My most fluent student Luis along with some of his friends, was explaining the importance and role in Chilean society that dancing has. As far as I recall he gave a brief overview of the main dance types, which ones were the most popular in the discotechas, and how that if you couldn't dance you weren't a real man, and would probably never lure any beautiful Chilean girls with your charms. After explaining all this he decided to ask me the dreaded question:

"How do people dance in England?"

The rest of the class immediately perked up, obviously expecting some sort of demonstration. Which is how I came to end up jerking around in front of the front of the class, in my best possible effort at 'grooving on down' in a Saturday night disco. During this time the atmosphere amongst my pupils changed from gleeful shiny-eyed enthusiasm, to one of shocked, open-mouthed silence.

This silence was only broken when Luis, eyebrows now deeply furrowed in a genuinely profound state of confusion, asked the question that must have been on the lips of every other person in the room:

"You mean......like....a puppet?"

It was therefore that I felt more than a little perturbed when told by my friend and mentor Lillian Gonzalez, that for September 18th I would have to learn the Cueca. She explained to me that there would be free classes every week at UFRO up until the time of the celebrations. Luckily for me however, help was to arrive in the form of Yohanna; a student of mine, and one of my best Chilean friends. An intelligent woman of Mapuche decent, she was very bright and a keen enthusiast of Chilean culture, her speciality being folkloric dance, and Cueca in particular.

Yohanna had accompanied me to several classes of Salsa and Merengie and had never given up trying to help me in my futile attempts to become the English equivalent of Ricky Martin. This was despite the many occasions on which I had almost simultaneously dislocated both her arms and broken her back, in moves that were more reminiscent of a drunken pub brawl than a smooth and alluring courtship dance. If I were to stand any chance of learning the Cueca in time for the

18th, a mere two weeks thence, I would need a woman of her substantial ability and infinite patience.

It was thus that I ended up in the UFRO gym hall, in a room packed with many other UFRO students keen to refresh their Cueca knowledge. Before the class began I bumped into quite a few familiar faces, some were RÜPÜ students, and others were friends of mine who I had got to know from time spent in the university mountaineering club.

I soon located Yohanna, then caught sight of Enzo Ferrari; a friend that I had got to know well in the mountaineering club. To this day I believe that Enzo is a man of deep thought and complex emotions, but a person wouldn't necessarily have realised this upon first meeting him. During my forays into the Andean mountains he had been one of several keen to instruct me in the ways of *'insolencia'*; a delightfully Chilean word that means 'foul language and bad behaviour'.

I had embraced his teachings with enthusiasm and soon could swear worse than a Chilean docker, and with more fluency than I could have a normal conversation. I had got on well with Enzo; someone who always seemed to display a tough exterior to all but his closest friends. But in the civilised atmosphere of the Cueca dance hall I naively hoped that what was said in the mountains, would stay in the mountains. But alas, I was to be disappointed.

"Hola Mother Fucker!" he proclaimed with glee upon seeing me standing there. And with that all hopes of me pretending to be a suave and sophisticated English gentleman vanished.

After the usual "como estas?' 'bien, y tu?' ritual he departed along with this girlfriend to a different part of the dance-floor, leaving me red faced and standing next to Yohanna in a state of genuine embarrassment, praying that she hadn't overheard.

"Who was that?" she asked, a look of consternation across her face.

"Just a friend…..erm did you hear?" I asked tentatively.

"Yes, such bad respect" she replied, her disapproval strongly evident by the tone of her voice.

It was at this point that my brain decided once again to rebel against me, for some reason feeling that to say anything was better than silence I declared:

"Don't worry, we always talk like that!"

The words had barely left my lips before I realised how bad they made me look, her only response being to say *"I see......"*

Splitting up, we all formed a large circle and the 40 or 50 of us began to dance round the room. I had already committed a cardinal sin even at this early stage by forgetting to bring a white hankie; something that forms an integral part of the ritual of the Cueca dance. Luckily for me another of my friends from the mountains; a kindly and adventurous chap called Boris, was on hand to lend me a black woollen glove that I was able to use as a poor substitute.

The opposite wall of the large dance hall was almost completely covered by a vast mirror; something that was probably a great aide to the majority of wannabe dance maestros, but for me only served to heighten the massive embarrassment factor, as I was able to watch my every awkward move reflected right back at me.

The Cueca dance is steeped in symbolism and is fundamentally based on a courting ritual between Rooster and Hen. The male plays the part of the domineering, almost aggressive Rooster, whilst the female part is based more on the role of the flirtatious and far from submissive Hen. In formal occasions the national dress is worn. The women wear elaborately patterned dresses often made of a white material embroidered with a red pink or yellow floral pattern, bordered occasionally by a frilly lace.

The men however adorn themselves with the costume of the Huaso; a type of cowboy and farmhand that although rare, can still be found in certain parts of Chile today. The costume comes in two forms. One is more elaborate than the other, but both contain the same basic elements; a large wide-brimmed hat, colourful poncho, a decorative shirt, and trousers rounded off with a pair of shiny silver spurs.

The white handkerchief is used by both the man and women throughout the dance. It is often whirled around the head in a display reminiscent of the mating rituals found throughout the animal kingdom, from the extravagant tail of the Peacock to the swollen red behind of the Baboon. The hankie, which can be anything from plain white to a much more elaborate embroidered and dyed variety, appears to represent the owner's virility and on the part of the male, also fulfils the role of a lasso with which to ensnare a potential mate.

The introductory practise now over, I was very pleased when Yohanna skipped over and asked me to dance. With her pleasant company and expert tuition it now mattered far less to me that everyone else in the room was seemingly wetting themselves with laughter at the ungainly gringo.

She proceeded to teach me that there are three stages to the Cueca; the first dance is where the male flirts and tries to conquer the female whilst she feigns disinterest. Then it is the woman's turn to flirt and try to ensnare the man that she desires. And in the third and final dance the two come together in harmony as the courting ritual reaches its conclusion.

All was going rather well. I was surprised to find that adapting to the scripted form of the Cueca was much easier than the random twists and twirls of salsa and meringue dancing. At one point I tried to inject some humour into the situation.

At the point where that male introduces himself to the girl and tries to charm her into dancing I rolled out one of the phrases taught to me by my RÜPÜ students, declaring; *"quieres bailar mijita rica?"*

Shocked and offended once again Yohanna backed away saying *"no, no, no way"* repeatedly. Only after a large amount of very humble and desperate begging on my part did she agree to continue with the cueca.

Later, at the point of the dance when I was obliged to produce my hankie, the very symbol of my status and masculinity and the centre-point of the Cueca itself, I could not for the life of me remember where I had put it. Desperately I patted down all my pockets as Yohanna watched with a look of utter bewilderment and disbelief. Eventually though I managed to rescue what remained of my dignity, locating the offending article and allowing our dance to continue.

There were many more pitfalls along the way, but the combination of classes and Yohanna's teachings, resulted in me becoming a semi-competent Cueca dancer by the time that September 18th arrived. At the end of that night I walked her through the darkened back streets of Temuco to the bus that led to her home; the riverside town of Pitrufquen that lay about 30km to the south.

***

Despite the frivolities of the Cueca classes and general Independence Day preparations, I was soon to be reminded that September in Chile is more complicated than a simple time of national celebrations. As with everything in Chile, where you encounter one extreme end of a spectrum, close by you are sure to find the other. In September when many are diligently preparing for the cheerful party atmosphere of the Independence Day celebrations, others are on the streets to 'commemorate' a different occasion; that of the September 11th military coup.

On the 9th of September I was coming towards the end of a three-hour Friday afternoon English class, teaching teens of high ability but in danger of social exclusion. Still working at UFRO, I had further expanded my English teaching resume by working as part of something called the Proenta Project.

Proenta was a special project designed to get the best out of bright kids; feeding their minds and talents and helping them to keep clear of trouble both in their homes and in their neighbourhoods. It was tough but rewarding work. Three hours is a long time to spend in a classroom on a Friday afternoon, and the young teenage students kept me on my toes with challenging questions that I often struggled to answer.

Most Fridays I then had to head straight on into the centre of town to one of the local colleges, where I helped the teachers with conversation and lesson planning. I would spend a few hours with two of the teachers correcting their pronunciation and clarifying points of grammar, before racing back to the university to spend a couple of hours climbing the indoor rock wall with RAUFRO.

Before all of this I had already taken classes at the beginning of the day in another university, before travelling to UFRO to teach several classes to the pupils of the RÜPÜ project.

So, by the time I arrived at home at ten or eleven on a Friday night, I was usually completely knackered. Often all that I was able to do was merely eat a meal and go straight to bed. But more often than not, my friends would hand me a few strong Piscolas, and ignoring my protests, manage to drag me out to the discotecas or bars downtown until five or six in the morning. It was an exhausting cycle of work and fun that repeated itself week after week.

That Friday was to be slightly different however. After wishing my young students the best for the weekend, I handed in my class registration at the Proenta office, and made my way towards the building's exit. But before I could depart I was accosted by the project leader who pulled me to one side.

With a genuinely concerned expression across her face, she warned me on no account to leave the university by the main or rear entrances. To my surprise she explained that there were 'battles' going on all around, and that it would be too dangerous for me to be out on the streets at such a time.

After telling her that I must leave as there were more classes that I needed to teach in the centre of the city, she reluctantly allowed me to leave by the side gate but cautioned me to be very careful.

Taking her advice, I located the small side gate and began to make my way to a point where I could catch the bus to the town centre. I soon found myself at a crossroads and it was decision time; turn left for the bus to town and my next job, or right up the road through the police barricades to the heart of where the disturbances were.

I had already had quite a few encounters with the violent protests and had been inadvertently tear gassed several times, but I had never seen them on a scale such as this before. I was curious to see more.

Decision made, I walked up the closed off dual carriage-way towards the police motorcycle blockade all the while trying my best to project an air of relaxed confidence, and a sense of determined purpose.

Stood resolutely across the road, the police seemed to be letting people pass who lived within the cordoned off area. I wound my way between the large, powerful and rugged motocross-style police bikes, and managed to walk on through with just a few sideways glances from the armour-clad officers. Up ahead I could see that the air was full of thick black smoke, from the many burning tyres in piles strewn across the road.

I soon arrived at a place close to the university gates adjacent to most of the burning tyres, and noticed that there were two main groups of protesters. The crowd nearest to me seemed to be nominally in charge of the operation, whilst the main group was further down the road and in sporadic conflict with the riot police in their staging area beyond.

Both groups were of the same appearance; plain clothes and heads that were shrouded in rags and balaclavas, which left only a thin slit to see through. They were devoid of any type banners or insignia; the sort of things that would usually be associated with a protest group.

Despite being stood out like a sore thumb, they seemed to be paying me little attention, and I was able to get quite close to the action. After about five minutes I decided to risk taking a photo. The protesters seemed very keen to keep their identities a secret, so I did my absolute best to be discreet about it. Holding the camera close to my chest and using the partial cover of a nearby lamppost, I held the camera as tight as I could and slowly depressed the shutter release.

Flicker, flicker flicker....flash!!! Went the flashgun as my heart leapt into my mouth! How could I have possibly been so stupid as to leave the flash on? A totally amateur mistake that could easily have cost me dearly. Luckily though few people seemed to have noticed, and there was no noticeable reaction from the 'protesters'.

It was at this point that my attention was drawn to the overhead power cables that criss-cross their way through the skies above Chile's streets. The electrical grid in Chile is distributed by means of these cables that weave their way over the city streets in a jumbled-looking entangled mess, attached to small overhead pylons. Many a time had I needed to sidestep my way around a dangling electrical cable, that I'd only spotted at the last moment as I'd been walking along the pavement.

They weren't buried beneath the ground apparently because of the high cost of installation, and due to the various natural disasters frequently suffered by the country; overhead cables are easier and quicker to replace and repair.

The relevance of this seemingly mundane fact, is that at this point several of the protesters began to gather up the rings of metal wiring which remain behind after a tyre has finished burning. They then hurled them up into the overhead power cables. This resulted in a blinding flash and shower of sparks, as the remaining street lights that were not already smashed faded into darkness. These protesters certainly seemed well practised in what they were doing.

Up until that point the police forces had shown incredible restraint. They had merely sealed off one end of the road with the aforementioned motorcycle blockade, and the other with their staging area, a line of drab green armoured vehicles to its fore. It seemed to me that the police tactics were merely to contain the disturbances. They responded to none of the provocations of the protesters, even when the infrastructure of the city was being destroyed. There was a good reason for their strict discipline; in a place with such a complicated social situation such as Temuco, the smallest of sparks could easily erupt into a full-on conflagration.

Despite surface appearances, the protesters were fighting for a cause. The cause varied depending on whom one was speaking to, from the cancellation of university fees for poor students, to proper equality for Mapuche people and the return of stolen Mapuche land. All these causes certainly had validity and were ones that the cash strapped Chilean state struggled to balance on a daily basis. An additional factor was that many

Latin American students err heavily on the left of the political spectrum, and tend to side with the underdog irrespective of the wider picture.

Had the police gone in heavy handed and arrested all the protesters, something that they were surely more than capable of doing, a wider and potentially far more serious situation could have developed involving much more of the local population than currently was the case. In fact, the regimented and practised way that the conflict seemed to be developing, bore close resemblance to the national Cueca dance. Gradually it unfolded as if adhering to a rehearsed formula, appearing random but at the same time being a routine that both sides had gone through dozens of times in the past, each faction playing out their role inside of where their boundaries lay.

As the first teargas grenade exploded metres from my feet I realized somewhat belatedly, that a white safari suite and a pair of Harry Potter spectacles, were probably not the best choice of attire to wear when attempting to pass myself off as a local, and blend inconspicuously into the background. I stood out like a sore thumb, amid what was rapidly developing into a violent riot.

Hurrying backwards towards the symbolic sanctuary of a battered steel bus stop, I avoided the brunt of the teargas effects, managing to escape with little more than an itchy throat and a pair of sore eyes.

One of the protestors suddenly ran forward. His shirt was held tightly against his face as he picked up and hurled the smoking tear gas canister back in the direction of the police lines. This act of defiance was reinforced by the teenager's friends who with screams of *"Paco Culiao!"* threw a cavalcade of heavy rocks towards the police vehicles.

This seemed to signify a turning point at which the intensity was turned up by everyone involved. Two armoured police 'Guanaco' water-cannon equipped riot trucks fired up their powerful engines, and began to speed down the street towards us. Red sirens flashed as they rumbled forward, their crews invisible behind windows shielded with steel mesh, and darkened by the shadows of the evening gloom.

By now the sun had now fully set. Its existence was only hinted at by a deep rosy-red hue to the far horizon.

111

As the Guanacos drew nearer the protesters fled towards the university gates. They climbed over and squeezed through the bars, desperate to get to the safe refuge beyond.

It was a rather odd peculiarity of the Chilean judicial system that the police had no standing authority to enter university premises, without prior consent of the chancellor. I have no idea how this arrangement came about, but it resulted in UFRO regularly becoming a fortified safe-haven for the type of protestors now battling in the street mere metres away.

Now safe behind the iron fence, the dissenting activists began to hurl volley after volley of rocks and petrol bombs, at the oncoming police vehicles.

Up until this point I had been observing from the side-lines standing across the other side of the road. Stood in the shadow of one of the street's ramshackle buildings and shrouded in the darkness of the blackened street, I had felt relatively safe. I was quietly confident in my pre-planned escape routes, should the situation turn sour and the need for a rapid exit arise.

Suddenly the pace of the battle intensified and my pulse quickened, as the air grew busy with sporadic flurries of rocks, tear gas grenades, petrol bombs and high-pressure water jets. One of the Guanacos made a bold charge towards the university, firing a roof-mounted water canon in bursts as it went. Rocks bounced off its armoured carapace as it inched closer and closer to the university gates. Just as it seemed inevitable that the Guanaco would impact the gates and throw them asunder, a bright fireball bloomed and engulfed the front half of it, to the accompanying sound of violently breaking glass.

The Guanaco was now ablaze with orange fire. Evidently a protestor had waited until the last minute before hurling his petrol bomb at point blank range. Bursting against the vehicle's bonnet, the bomb had shattered, causing flaming petrol to pour down and engulf the front wheels, igniting the tyres in the process. This sudden assault caused the police to withdraw to a safer area, giving the now jubilant teenagers some breathing room.

The skirmish was to continue back and forth in this manner for much of the night, a cycle of tear gas and petrol bombs repeating itself as if it were a strange courtship dance.

This was one of many such encounters during my time in Temuco. Sometimes I would be caught in them by accident, but as the weeks passed by I would increasingly head out on purpose. Armed with a camera and wearing a cap pulled down low over my eyes, I would try to get close to the action.

On one occasion I was starting out on one of my regular half-hour walks into town, making my way down the dusty, neglected side streets that passed between the side of the university and a disused railway line. Unaware of anything untoward happening, and about half a mile away from the usual danger epicentre, I continued forwards in blissful ignorance, concerned with nothing but the scorching midday heat. It wasn't long though before I felt a persistent tickle at the back of my throat. Assuming it to be dust from the street, I tried to clear it with a cough. This didn't work and before long I could feel a prickly tingling sensation on my skin and eyes. This rapidly grew in intensity and I soon realised that it was not a figment of my imagination.

It wasn't long before I was coughing and choking. As I stumbled forwards with eyes closed to a squint and skin stinging as if in contact with a chemical irritant, I noticed that the few other people in the street at the time were suffering similarly. The realisation dawned on me that a cloud of teargas must have been blown from the scene of the troubles and dispersed by the wind. It had travelled through the air until it fell once more to ground, in the area through which I was now attempting to pass.

By now I couldn't open my eyes at all, and when I tried I found them so full of tears that I could see nothing. Despite trying my best to maintain my composure my eyes and nose were now streaming, and I was coughing constantly. I had to get out of the area.

Staggering along the dusty street and unable to see, I tried to resist the urge to rub the gas out of my eyes. I must have looked quite a sight as I scuffed my feet along the floor, eyes streaming with tears as I tried to feel my way out of the danger zone. It is a rather surreal and bewildering experience to be idly going about your normal business once minute, then to be engulfed in an invisible cloud of tear gas of unknown origin the next.

Eventually the bodily fluids streaming from my face won the struggle against the chemical irritant, and I began to see clearly again. Once clear of the gas cloud I saw other Chileans nearby with similarly tear-smeared faces. One of them; a young woman, caught my eye,

and gave me a kindly smile accompanied with a shrug
in a 'shit happens in Chile' gesture of solidarity.

Mountains and Wetlands

Despite not having been in Chile a great length of time, I was gradually getting the hang of the language and beginning to make friends amongst my students. At the same time I was managing to earn an income that allowed me to be self-sufficient, so long as my only requirements continued to be rent, food and alcohol.

I still needed quite a lot of help from my good friend Lillian, but I found that I was no longer totally dependent on her as was the case for the first month or two. However, just as I thought I'd settled in to a kind of routine, I enjoyed a week that was to blow away all that I'd experienced thus far and change the course of my life forever.

For the previous few months I'd been meeting up regularly with the University of the Frontier mountain

117

climbing group. This was a group of adventurous students who united under the title of the 'Rama de Andinismo' (Club of the Andes) or RAUFRO for short. It was a tightly knit club willing to attempt any challenge regardless of difficulty, hardship, weather or altitude. Their expeditions were as varied as Chile's geography would allow, but a common factor was that most involved scaling heights that many mountain goats would baulk at.

The group was led by a strong and determined young woman called Paula Guarda. Her gleaming smile and boundless enthusiasm for the outdoors, was an inspiration for generations of youngsters from all backgrounds to take up mountaineering. Paula not only helped me to learn skills for the mountains, but also Spanish and Chilean culture. These were things for which I would be forever in her debt.

Despite being a strange foreigner I was warmly welcomed into their world, and had already accompanied them on several entertaining excursions. I was therefore very interested, when I heard that they had managed to organize a course run by the commando regiment of the Chilean Army, of mountain skills and survival. It was to take part in the high Andes mountains in just a couple of weeks' time.

The Chilean peoples' relationship with their army is quite an unusual one, and is something that has been shaped by several events which have taken place over the last few decades. For many people in the west, if they have heard of Chile at all, it is because of the infamous military dictatorship headed by General Augusto José Ramón Pinochet, who held power between the years of 1973 and 1990. The military led by the army under Pinochet, seized power in a violent military coup which had tacit political backing from the United States, on September 11th 1973.

The coup ousted the increasingly unpopular socialist government led by Salvador Allende; the first socialist president of Chile. In the final hours of the takeover, battles raged across Santiago between the military and Allende's dwindling band of supporters. As troops began to storm his presidential palace, Allende barricaded himself inside, and managed to transmit by radio what would become his final address to the nation:

"Workers of my country, I have faith in Chile and its destiny. Other men will overcome this dark and bitter moment when treason seeks to prevail. Keep in mind that, much sooner than later, the great avenues will again be opened through which will pass free men to construct a better society. Long live Chile! Long live the people! Long live the workers!"

Shortly after delivering this speech he was dead. According to various sources he committed suicide, having shot himself with a gun given to him as a gift by his close friend Fidel Castro; the then revolutionary president of Cuba.

Upon his election, Allende had conducted a series of sweeping socialist reforms that whilst initially popular, were to prove disastrous for the country's economy. As the situation worsened there were large scale union strikes, civil unrest, the breakdown of basic public services, and a drastic reduction in the quality of life for the average Chilean.

In addition to this, relations with the United States fell to an all-time low. This was partly due to the very fact that Allende was a socialist, but also due to US fears of increasing Communist and Soviet influence in Latin America. This souring of US relations and subsequent direct involvement of the CIA, was to prove a powerful catalyst to the destabilization of Chile's economy and the subsequent social upheavals.

It would be unfair to place all the blame for Chile's woes solely on Allende's shoulders, especially when considering that he came to power as a result of free and fair elections. It could however be said that it was his government's over enthusiastic reforms, coupled with its communist sympathies, that made him powerful enemies in the White House. This in turn made conditions ripe in the winter of 1973 for the military to move in and take charge. After a brief assault by the army on La Moneda ('The Coin' as the presidential place in central Santiago is known), supported by bombing runs by the Air-Force, the military were soon in control. Democracy in Chile for the time being, was a thing of the past.

The ruling junta immediately set about consolidating their power, by eliminating as many of the perceived left-wing opposition as possible. In the following seventeen years the dictatorship would have a significant impact on all aspects of life for most of the population. It would leave around 3000 people dead or 'disappeared', and a further 27,000 imprisoned, along with many cases of physical abuse and horrific torture. A perhaps more significant impact was the one on the national psyche. The era of the dictatorship imparted upon the populace a general aura of oppression, the aftershocks of which are still palpable in some sections of society to this day.

There is however another side to the coin. For many people the Pinochet era is directly responsible for Chile being described in some quarters as 'the Latin American miracle'. This is due to the widespread and far reaching economic reforms, that he instigated in the years following his rise to power. He enlisted the help of the Chicago Boys; a skilled group of economic advisors from the United States, who helped stabilise the economy and lay the financial foundations from which Chile benefits today. This made Chile a prosperous and relatively stable democracy, at a time when the rest of the continent was being torn apart by internal strife, civil conflict and economic collapse.

The Pinochet issue is one that remains highly controversial in Chilean public opinion, and is a subject on which many Chileans are often very reluctant to express their thoughts, especially to a foreigner. But as with most things, there is a spectrum of opinion between two extremes.

On one hand the reforms and economic management put in place by Pinochet's administration, saved Chile and its people from the concurrent disasters that wracked most of the other nations of Latin America. They left a legacy of a prosperous economy, that to this day remains a shining example of what is possible south of the equator, under the right conditions. Chile's current economic prosperity has without doubt led directly to a better standard of living, for all who dwell within her borders. However, this is felt far more by those at the higher end of the financial spectrum than by those at the bottom.

It may therefore be possible to understand views that General Augusto Pinochet is in fact a national hero; a man whose devotion to duty, and powerful leadership, has led to perhaps the only notable success story on the South American continent. Chileans benefit from a far superior standard of living to those in nearby Argentina, Peru, Bolivia and Brazil, and significantly they are not afflicted by the appallingly high levels of corruption that still plague those nations. It has a well-trained and utterly devoted armed forces. There is a well-organized and disciplined (if a little authoritarian) government, police and justice system, and the country is united by a sense of national unity and pride that must rank among the highest in the world.

However, like most things in life all this has come at a price. The price has been very high indeed, and is one steeped in blood, pain, oppression and suffering. Upon seizing power in September 1973, the ruling military junta immediately set about consolidating their power via a process achieved with clinical precision, and utter ruthlessness.

Their first objective was to eliminate as much of the serious left-wing opposition as possible. This was achieved through assassination, intimidation, and 'disappearance'; a word that often signified abduction followed by torture and execution. Even those not involved with politics could not express their opinions to anyone but closest family members, living in constant fear of being reported to, and subsequently disappeared by, the notorious DINA; Pinochet's infamous secret

124

police. The following is an extract given from an Amnesty International mission to Chile:

"The most common physical tortures described in testimonies available to Amnesty International were: beating; administration of electric shocks and burns on the head and sensitive parts of the body; rape and other sexual abuse of women; non-therapeutic use of drugs; sleep deprivation... 'la parrilla', the metal grill, consisting of electric shocks on the most sensitive parts of the victim's body (usually the genitals, mouth, temples, toes, wrists) while he or she is tied to a metal bed frame...."[2]

The report goes on in more depth, detailing some of the horrendous tortures used, that were on a par with those from the concentration camps of Nazi Germany. Of particular discomfort to me was reading about those used on the female detainees. There exists a large amount of further information on this subject. Some of it is objective, some with clear bias, but I don't believe it to be appropriate to reproduce here in the context of this account.

Those in support of the regime, will argue that most of those treated in such a manner would have been involved in or associated with terrorism. This indeed is a side that is never represented in the media. It is very hard to find numbers for the amount of police and soldiers who were surely killed and maimed by rebels, whilst innocently serving their communities. It is often too easy to take the side of obvious victims, unimaginable though their suffering has been, without trying to comprehend the broader picture.

Taking this troubled past into consideration, a person could be justified in assuming that the Chilean people's opinion of their armed forces must be a deeply negative one, especially when considering the common knowledge that much of the army still holds loyalties to the former General. However Chile retains a system of national conscription, with much of the nation's youth having served in the Army for at least a year. These young conscripts are the sons, brothers and fathers of families from across a nation, where families are very closely knit by nature.

Being a country of such geographic extremes and devastating natural disasters, Chile relies on its military to frequently rescue, house and feed a populace struck by everything from tsunamis and earthquakes, to snowstorms and civil unrest. Walk the streets for any period in the cities of Chile's south, and you are sure to see many uniformed green or red-bereted soldiers, going about their daily business. They are as much a part of daily life as the roadside fruit sellers. This, along with the large numbers of disciplined carabiñeros ever present, instils a deep sense of order and safety, even if the reality doesn't always quite live up to appearances.

This is not to say that there aren't many people who despise the military, as there are many who do, some with very good reason. But hopefully this may go some way to help you the reader understand why the events that I'm about to describe were such a deep tragedy, and a subject that is still capable of bringing tears to my eyes today.

***

On the day before the mountain survival course, I woke up early at a seemingly ungodly hour in the morning, leaving the house in complete darkness. Weighed down by my large pack, I met up with the rest of the team from RAUFRO, before taking the coach to the local army regiment.   On arrival we entered the base and the coach turned around, as some of the group joked that I should close my eyes so that I didn't see all of the Chilean military secrets. We were joined by the rest of our party, before an army officer came on board and wished us all the best.

The coach then departed on what was to become a journey of over two hours, to the small mountain town of Lonquimay. As the morning sun rose above the horizon, the spectacular beauty of the surrounding landscape was revealed to me in all its splendour. The weather was fantastic, and the views were incredible.

I saw the volcanoes called Llaima and, Lonquimay, and the Sierra Nevada mountain range up close, as well as many more mountains. Beyond these, in the far distance was Volcan Villarrica, emitting a thin column of smoke which was spread in a thin line across the eastern sky, pointing like an arrow to the north. An omen perhaps, but whether it was one for good or bad I was yet to discover.

Eventually we left the Pan Americana and the road wound its way eastwards. After passing through some very impressive foothills the terrain became more and more mountainous, until eventually we were confronted by a sheer, ice-glazed wall of granite. At the bottom of this was the comparatively small entrance to the longest road tunnel in South America. It was called Las Raices, and after entering the tunnel portal we emerged once more into daylight after about five minutes of steady driving.

The scene which confronted us upon leaving the tunnel was a stark contrast to the one which we had just left behind. We had arrived in an eerie snow-covered mountain world, where the clouds shrouded the valley floor hundreds of metres below. The coach continued to make its way higher and higher and the chatter amongst our party gradually became more subdued, as we edged our way along the thin road high up on the glacial valley wall.

As time passed by, the clouds which were blocking sight of the deep valley floor gradually burnt off with the mid-morning sun. The already grand scale of the area that we were entering was now fully revealed in all of its glory. After a while the road began to descend, and signs of human habitation begin to appear. Before long we entered the outer limits of the small mountain town of Lonquimay.

It was immediately apparent that the populace of such a remote place must live with a great deal of hardship. The sheep and cows all sported immense coats of thick wool, reminiscent of the highland cattle of Scotland. Most of the fields were buried under at least a foot of snow. The houses were all of wooden construction as was the norm in the south of Chile, with most being single story dwellings. However, there were a few rickety two-storey edifices, and it was next to one of these that our coach pulled up.

As we disembarked we were greeted by two soldiers from the local regiment. Both were much taller than the average Chilean, and they seemed to be much more heavily built than most of the conscripts I was used to seeing around the streets of Temuco. One of them had a particularly battered complexion, brought on by a prolonged exposure to the harsh mountain climate. His face had been reddened by a mixture of sunburn and the sharp bite of the harsh mountain winds.

On his head the man wore a black woollen hat emblazoned with the word 'commando' in gold lettering, he also sported parachute wings sewn onto the shoulders of his jacket. At the top of his chest were the two standard patches with which most Chilean soldiers are adorned; Ejercito De Chile on the left breast, and his surname, Pizanni on the right. After a quick group photo, we went inside the billet to claim a bed each and drop off our bags.

Despite the cosy appearance of the two-storey building that was to be our home for the next six days, the interior left a lot to be desired. The main living room was devoid of furnishings except for a small battered couch, and an iron wood-burning stove in one corner. Being one of the first into the dormitory, I chucked my pack onto the top bunk of one of the beds closest to the door. I then began to unpack some things as my course-mates filed in around me.

I use the word bed in its loosest possible connotation. It was really just a very thin wire frame with a rectangle of foam placed on the top. There was a very suspiciously smelling blanket, which I choose to place under my sleeping bag rather than on top of it. Although I didn't realize it at the time, choosing the top bunk had been a major stroke of good fortune. I was only about 2ft below the ceiling, and therefore was to gain a valuable amount of extra heat during the night when it was radiated from one of the nearby dangling light-bulbs.

We'd barely had time to take account of where we were, before being whisked off to the nearby army base of Regimiento Nº 8 "Tucapel". Tucapel had been the name of a legendary Mapuche hero and warrior who had fought fiercely against the Spanish conquistadors some centuries ago. Next followed a long period standing outside waiting. Some of us sensibly spent this time sleeping out in the winter sun, but I wasn't particularly tired, so was able to pass the time taking in the spectacular local scenery.

The inhabitants of that mountain base must surely have been made of quite stern stuff, as there were no home comforts that I could see. It was located on the outskirts of the village of Lonquimay; a lonely hamlet with a significant Mapuche population. It was made up of a series of unimpressive tin huts which had been painted in a rudimentary black and green camouflage pattern. The huts functioned as dormitories, washrooms, kit stores and an armoury. The soldiers' dormitory seemed of only marginally better quality the digs that we had been given down in the town, the main difference being that we were only there for six days, whilst the soldiers were stationed there for significantly longer. The other major building was the mess hall, in which we were treated to pleasant, if basic meals throughout our stay.

Once the long period of waiting was over, we were ushered into one of the tin buildings for our initial preparation. This took the form of a briefing and a demonstration of some of the equipment that we would be using throughout the course. Particularly unnerving was the explanation of the two different types of avalanche rescue equipment, avalanches being a very serious threat in the region.

The first type was a two-way adjustable range radio beacon, which a person should activate upon being overwhelmed be an avalanche. Voice communication in such a situation would not be possible, so the victim had to instead rely on the other team members to locate him using their own beacons. Each man would narrow down the range on their receiver as the signal strengthened, until they got close to the position of the victim and could then begin to dig like crazy.

If this technique failed or was unavailable there was a second option. This consisted of a soldier with what was basically just a long metal pole, that would be continually poked down into the snow until it connected with a solid object, i.e. a body. The pole could be lengthened up to a total length of four metres. It was this technique that I witnessed being used night after night on the news, during the Antuco disaster.

They called it a 'snow tsunami', and it had struck in an area close to the isolated Antuco volcano. At that time of year Temuco was being swamped by a deluge of torrential autumn rains. Many of the city's major streets were knee-deep in water, as the drainage systems became overwhelmed block by block.

At that point in my Chilean journey I still had not started work properly due to the large amount of ongoing student unrest. I was spending my time desperately trying to improve my Spanish, but finding the required studying boring and uninspiring. One way that I did find to stimulate my interest was to pay close attention to the local evening news. This was often particularly entertaining as I was frequently to see on the news places that I had been that very same day, not something I had ever been able to say back home in England.

One night I returned from work to find that a big story was breaking. This was evident from the dramatic pictures emanating from the television set in Ale's parents' bedroom. It seemed that there were a significant number of troops from the region just to the north of Temuco, which were on an exercise deep within the mountains. Four hundred and thirty-three soldiers, many of whom young conscripts, had been out training on the formidable Antuco volcano, when they were suddenly hit by a fearsome storm of whirling snow.

The majority had managed to make it to safety, but ninety-five were still lost and as every hour passed by the situation became increasingly desperate. Soon the first bodies were to be brought out. Most seemed to have lain down in the snow out of utter exhaustion, intending to rest for just a few minutes. They were never to wake up. Having some experience of being cold and tired in the mountains myself, I had known the urge to 'just lie down in the snow and rest for a while'. Fortunately I had never been in such dire straits as to give into the temptation.

Bodies frozen in a variety of ridged poses, many of the young soldiers appeared as if they were merely sleeping, whilst from the pained expressions on the faces of others, it was clear that the end for them had been far less peaceful.

Gradually some more survivors managed to make their way out, and as they did so families of the men still lost packed the local regimental barracks, desperate for any news of their sons and brothers. Unfortunately, the tales that the survivors had brought with them were not uplifting ones. Many spoke of being so exhausted, freezing and lost, that they had been forced to abandon their colleagues where they lay to stand any chance of escape. Such a dilemma is the stuff of nightmares; having to decide whether to drag their friends with them and almost certainly die alongside them, or leave their doomed and failing bodies to the elements in order to have at least a minute chance of survival.

After a few agonizing days for all of the families involved, all but forty-five men had staggered down from the mountains. But by this time it seemed to me that there could be no hope for those that remained, they must surely all be dead. The military was still insisting to the contrary, and was to continue to do so for another three days. Apart from seeing the footage on TV of the hellish conditions and bodies frozen in agony, what really brought the tragedy of the situation home to me was watching the anguish of the families.

The news was full for weeks of mothers, fathers, sisters, brothers and children, crying and screaming as they waited in a bare gymnasium hall, for even the slightest glimmer of any good news. Each of them held onto a desperate hope that their son or brother might soon by some miracle come walking in through the door.

News media in the west is rather bland in comparison. It is impossible to get a true appreciation of the human impact of natural disasters, famines and wars from a few sanitised video clips accompanied by the monotone narrative of a remote and disconnected newsreader. But it brought a knot to my stomach every night, watching those mothers cry and scream for their sons whilst I knew in my heart that they would not be coming home alive.

Many of these young conscripts had been from very poor families, and some had joined the Army only a month before this tragic event. For many mothers those boys had been the only source of hope in a cruel world; brightening up their families' lives with smiles and jokes, and making poverty just a little more bearable. The search efforts would continue for another few weeks, but the weather conditions remained horrendous, so the going was difficult and incredibly slow. But by the 6th of July, the last of the bodies had been recovered. The remaining forty-five soldiers had all perished.

It was not long before accusations started to fly. The primary one being that of negligence by the army officers; for sending their troops out in such conditions and poorly equipping them to deal with the weather that had struck them. It is true that the suddenness and ferocity of that fatal storm was exceptional. But it is easy to say with hindsight that such a tragedy could have been avoided. If nothing else, these events were a real lesson to me on the great responsibilities of command, and the respect that must always be had for a malevolent mother nature.

Back in the Lonquimay base, our avalanche rescue demonstration was coming to an end. It was a sobering thought that the instructor demonstrating the rescue equipment to us, must have seen it used just weeks before to locate the frozen corpses of his colleagues and friends, beneath the desolate area around the Antuco volcano. It was this that despite the frequently jovial atmosphere of the group, brought down to earth the significance of what we were doing and where we were going, and the importance that we must succeed without mishaps.

The importance of this to me was threefold. Firstly I felt that every man who died so horribly over those few days would want people to continue in their footsteps. I also harboured the belief that when mother nature demonstrates the true severity of her wrath, she must be fought head on and given no quarter, until there is either no possibility of further resistance or she tires of inflicting further suffering upon her victims. The third and final reason that I considered the success of this week to be of paramount importance, was that the honour of the soldiers of Chile is something I had a high regard for, and I wanted to prove myself worthy of their respect.

Despite the controversy attached to Chile's recent military history, these soldiers were men who were patriotic almost to a level of fanaticism and, if necessary would have died for the country that they love. They were certainly not saints, and many may have had political views that would repulse more liberal minded people, but their intentions were good, and, I believe their souls pure. Therefore, I endeavoured to try my hardest to ensure that all would go as planned, and that the Chilean Army could take a group of total novices into the high mountains and bring them back, twice the people that they were before.

We were shown the rest of the kit, which seemed to be of very good quality. Camouflaged coveralls were made of Gore-Tex, and clearly built for the mountains. There was also a backpack that was an excellent large mountain design. The label on the sleeping bag said that it was suitable for temperatures as low as –40ºC, and was 'comfortable' down to -25ºC.

The afternoon was spent watching a short film about the Ejercito (army) and listening to lectures on mountain survival, dangers and illnesses. We were shown some rather grisly photos of three stages of frostbite, and given lessons on some of the major mountain hazards.

We were taught that all the potential problems fitted into one of two categories of causation; subjective, which are inherent in the person (usually manifested in an unsuitable character or a lack of preparation), and objective; which are problems inherent in the mountains, and often beyond human control. We then proceeded to learn about more specific medical issues in-depth, including some gruesome photos of what an open fracture could look like.

I understood most of what was being said, as I already had a slight interest in the topic. Many of the words were technical or medical terms which were similar to the English ones. After a long day, I headed off to the Billet and after a bit of chatter and preparation of kit, fell into a deep sleep ready for the day to come.

We awoke to a bracingly cold Tuesday morning. Putting on our boots and shouldering our skis, we boarded a battered but reliable Mercedes army truck, and headed up into the mountains east of the Lonquimay Volcano for a day of ski randonee training.

Ski randomee is a type of skiing known in the West as cross country skiing. It involves the use of specially adapted skis that allow you to march uphill over snow. They have a type of one-way carpet fitted underneath, that most of the time allows the ski to slide forwards easily while resisting slippage backwards. We had been split up into small groups which each were made up of one instructor and four students. My group consisted of Boris; the gent who lent me his glove during the cueca dancing class, and two other lads, both called Rodrigo.

Our instructor for the next two days was to be a man called Gonzalez, who appeared to be significantly older than the other instructors and soldiers that I had so far seen. The army was apparently his lifelong career. He had an easy-going, friendly attitude, and an avuncular vibe that immediately endeared us to him.

After skiing off for a bit to distance ourselves from the other groups, Gonzalez demonstrated a strange slide and walk technique to us. It involved detaching the boot heel clamps and sliding the ski forwards with the toes, then transferring the body weight onto the leading foot whilst the back foot is brought forwards in the same manner. We then strapped on our large mountain 'mochilas' (rucksacks), and headed off deeper into the surrounding mountains.

The constant methodical transferring of body weight from one foot to the other took a while to master, but it was not too long before we were moving along quite competently.

I soon got into my stride and really began to enjoy ski randomee. It was far easier than hiking, even with snow shoes, and I barely noticed the weight of the mochila on my back. We stopped for a break and I offered Gonzalez a sip from my canteen. Politely refusing, he commented that I was obviously absorbing the camaraderie that the mountains tend to imbue. I considered this a little overly dramatic, but it started me thinking about how vital team work was in an arena such as this.

After just a few kilometres it began to feel that we really were in the wilderness. There were no trails, no footprints, and we were far out of sight of the ski centre. The weather was incredibly clear, and as we ascended I caught a glimpse of the tip of the Lonquimay volcano poking up above the mountains. It was not the most symmetrically beautiful volcano I had ever seen, but still was an awesome sight. I still hadn't put on my sun goggles or 'anti-paras' as they were known, because the snow did not seem to be particularly bright. But I soon started to feel a tingling, sort of burning feeling in my eyes, so I slapped them on as quickly as possible. I was not rapid enough however, and it took at least two minutes for the pain to subside, and for my eyes to stop streaming with tears. I resolved not to make the same mistake again.

Gonzalez then mentioned that he was going to show us an area prone to avalanches. I may be mistaken, but it did seem at the time that he pointed out to us a section of slope that was unstable and had all the characteristics of a potential avalanche site, and then proceeded to lead us skiing right over the top of it! It was certainly one way to get used to the perils of the mountains.

We ascended even higher, and the going suddenly became very difficult. Up until this point I'd encountered no problems. In fact I had been the only member of the team bar the instructor not to have fallen over, slid down a ravine or, piled straight into a tree. But here the gradient was very steep, and the snow was hard, compacted down and slippery, almost like ice.

No matter how much weight I put on my front foot I just couldn't get any grip. After falling over countless times and almost sliding down the mountain, I eventually made it past the difficult section thanks to my friends using their 'bastones' (ski-poles) to anchor my skies after every single step. On the way up I tried to stamp down the snow a lot more, to make it easier for those behind me.

After this relatively minor difficulty we made it to the top of the ridge that was to be the site of our lunchtime base camp. The views were spectacular, and no photos could possibly do them justice. Until you have seen mountains like this, you can't really appreciate why photos just don't cut the mustard. There is no way that a picture on its own can possibly relate the true scale and vastness of the location.

Blessed with clear skies, we could see an immeasurable distance. Our vision was only blocked by the high Andes to the east, on the border with Argentina. Curiously, earlier on in my Chilean adventures I had a great deal of trouble judging the distance of mountains and volcanoes, because I had never encountered anything on their scale before. I could not understand why everyone was laughing, when I had said that I intended to walk to the volcano that I could see from Ale's farm. The volcano I had guessed was about ten kilometres away. I now know that their mirth was due to it being over two hundred kilometres distant, or a two-hour journey by coach.

Meanwhile the other groups had been doing much the same thing, accompanied by their own individual instructors. Later I was to learn that a team containing a friend of mine; the amicable and approachable Victor and his girlfriend Rosa, had been even higher than we were. They had managed to summit the high ridge above our lunch-break position, where they were presented with incredible views of the surrounding mountains, distant volcanoes, and the rare natural phenomena of a cloud formation making its way up the opposite side of the ridgeline, before breaking over the top as the skiers made their ascent.

We ate lunch atop the high ridgeline and washed it down with a welcome dose of hot coffee from our instructor's thermos. Unbeknownst to us whilst we sat there in that tranquil spot was that our real troubles were about to begin, as we got our first experience of skiing downhill. Following Gonzalez' lead, we began to head downhill via a slope that was rather steep, and seemed to be very 'off-piste'. It seemed quite an extraordinarily dangerous place to have our first ever skiing lesson.

It was apparent that our instructor believed that the proverbial deep end was the best place to learn. At one point I seemed to be helplessly skiing very slowly towards the edge of a sheer cliff, that must have been at least 100m high. Just the mere idea that I might not be able to stop myself from being destined to head slowly and inexorably towards a long fall followed by a messy death, was enough to bring a real sense of terror to the pit of my stomach!

After successfully steering myself away from this obstacle, I proceeded to fall over dozens of times, and was unable to progress more than five metres at any one time before landing flat on my face again. I really got an appreciation of just how easy it is to break limbs while skiing. Luckily I have always been surprisingly flexible, something that is a considerable benefit when both of your legs decide to head in completely opposite directions at a high speed!

Up to this point I had been swearing mildly at any mishaps in Castellano, using the mild term of chuta! (damn), or sometimes the slightly stronger version;

chucha (bloody hell!). I discovered though that when things go really wrong, a natural return to one's native language is inevitable.

This was to occur when I was skiing merrily down the slope, feeling like I was just getting the hang of things. Then suddenly my skis crossed, then separated, followed by my legs heading in completely different and highly unnatural directions. This was followed by me gaining an entirely unwanted insight into how the term 'pelvic fracture' was developed, all accompanied to the sound of; *"hm hmm hm hmm, chucha!!! Shit! Shit! Fuuuuuck!!!!!!"*

The only saving grace was that there weren't any members of the public around, to question why the unusually tall and white Chilean specialist mountain soldier, not only could not ski, but also chose to swear out loud in a foreign nation's language.

We continued down the mountain, and I was determined not to be the last out of our small team. Then just as I seemed to be getting the hang of things, one of my skis came loose on a particularly steep slope. It was this ski on which the safety chord; the chord that attaches the ski to the leg to avoid losing it, was a little broken.

Therefore I had to resign myself to watching helplessly, as the ski glided extremely gracefully sideways down the mountain. It ended its journey in a clump of trees clustered in the bottom of a valley. It was a little depressing that it seemed to possess a far better ability to ski by on its own, than when hindered by my ineptitude.

I shouldered my remaining ski and pointed down the mountain-side to indicate to Gonzalez where I would be heading on my walk of shame. The trek didn't actually take all that long, and I was soon reunited with my wayward ski. I reattached it to my boot and then Nordic skied back up the slope to reunite with my team.

When I caught up with them they were waiting at the bottom of a small slope, which I hiked up and started to ski back down. Seeing this sudden spark of potential ability, Gonzalez commented with a grin; *"muy bien Tom"*.

However, I had not yet figured out how to actually stop whilst skiing. So, as I drew level with him I propelled myself sideways and proceed to land in a crumpled heap. I ended up half buried face down in the compacted snow, barely one metre from his camouflage shrouded legs.

"Y un muy buen para Tom!" (and a very good stop tom) he exclaimed, whilst bursting out into a fit of jovial laughter.

Apart from skiing down a very big hole, and afterwards straight into a tree, then another tree, then a very big hole with a tree in it, the rest of the day's training went fairly well.

So well in fact, that by the time we reached the end my confidence was high enough to ski past the other members of the squad, shouting, *"Y en primero posición: Inglaterra!!!"*.

Unfortunately my glorious and sudden burst of confidence was to be short lived. Not looking properly where I was going, I finished my run by skiing directly into yet another tree, one that proved to be considerably more solid and spiky than I.

As the day drew to a close we made our way back to the Army truck, then climbed aboard ready for the trip back to base. All of us were in very high spirits after such a successful day, so the whole journey back was characterised by raucous singing, games and general high-spirits.

I was asked by the group if I could sing some songs that I knew. But as I looked around the suddenly quiet interior of the packed truck at the 20 or so pairs of expectant eyes around me, my mind went totally blank. I was unable to recall of a single English song. To my shame my non-English-speaking companions seemed to know far more songs in English than I did.

Back at the base we ate a big and nutritious dinner together. Following this, some of the 'rougher' members of our team, led by Enzo Ferrari and his friend Luis, decided to give me an impromptu lesson in Chilean 'insolencia'. This was a term that meant bad behaviour, but in this case it involved Enzo and his pals teaching me the most appallingly foul swear words and rude phrases in the Chilean language, then falling about in fits of laughter as I repeated them in my 'posh' English accent.

I decided to take a shower, and it was then that we discovered that there seemed to be no hot water. After searching the house from top to bottom, no gas for the water heater could be found. So a cold shower it was to be. After stepping naked into the concrete trench that served as a shower, I looked upwards with apprehension at the small, corroded showerhead. Considering that the road outside was speckled with lumps of ice and snow, I braced myself for what was about to hit me.

Taking a deep breath, I gripped the tap and span it around as rapidly as possible. The water then gushed out of the pipe at a ferocious rate, and my scream of:

"Aaarrrrgh bloody hell!" could probably have been heard back in Temuco.

This was followed by a round of giggling from the other guys in the bathroom, and by Enzo sticking his head around the rough concrete shower wall, and remarking with a laugh:

"Is it a bit cold Tom?"

To which the only reply I could give in Spanish in my freshly learned insolencia was; *"it's absolutely fucking freezing!!"*

I stood there hyperventilating, with my manhood trying its utmost to retreat all the way back into my body in some sort of emergency last ditch hibernation attempt. But I gradually became accustomed to the cold, and soon a bizarre sensation of warmth swept over me as my body fought to regain a sense of thermal equilibrium. Soon enough I finished my shower, and it was then my turn to laugh at the screaming of the other participants of 'operation hypothermia shower'.

Before bedtime the more energetic of us decided to head out for a night on the town. Unfortunately though, it soon became apparent that Lonquimay was certainly not Chile's most happening tourist resort.

Our enthusiastic questions of *"dónde es la discotec?"* were met with nothing but bemused laughter from the local population, so we had to assume by this that there wasn't one.

Failing to find a pub or even a ramshackle cantina[1] we ended up in the village's sole small restaurant, and then helped the proprietors to create more empty space in their already rather spartan beer fridge.

---

[1] A drinking establishment usually frequented by the poorer members of the populace, where cheap beer and cigarettes may be taken lit by a dim bulb in the barest of surroundings.

My drinking companions took this opportunity to teach me one more lesson, and thanks to my poor performance on the Army truck, it was to come in the form of learning two songs. The first was the Chilean national anthem, and the second was the following:

"Haciendo el amor....haciendo el amor....

toda la noche.....

Juntitos los dos, haciendo el amor.....toda la noche......"[1]

You probably had to be there, but when accompanied with the appropriate hand gestures it was to be of great benefit to me as a tool to entertain, and a source of amusement to fellow passengers on future truck journeys.

_____

[1] *Making love…. Making love*

All night long

The two of us together, making love…. All night long

After a short but deep sleep, we were woken an hour earlier than planned, by Chilean military marching music that emanated from the floorboards above my head at a deafening volume. The previous day a platoon of soldiers had arrived from Temuco to take part in a winter skiing and shooting competition, and they had taken up residence upstairs. We assumed that the music was their payback for us coming back late, drunk and noisy the night before. We managed to see the funny side though.

It was in fact not actually all that bad a way to wake up, and I somehow managed to wrench myself from the warn cocoon of my sleeping bag and get out of bed. After getting dressed and collecting all our kit, we wandered over to the camp for breakfast.

The breakfasts on the camp seemed surprisingly small considering that they were for soldiers, especially when bearing in mind the familiar saying that an army marches on its stomach. After the meal we piled once again into the back of the old army truck, and headed up the steep track into the surrounding mountains.

I was sat near to the tailgate, and was thrown about like a cat in a washing machine as I tried to take in the views of picturesque snow-covered farms, and the incredibly hardy cattle that somehow managed to dwell on them. On the way up we gave a lift to a local kid who seemed to know the soldiers quite well. I never got his name, but he didn't look much over 13 years old, and was to accompany us for the remainder of the day.

After debussing at the ski centre we split off into our different groups. My group was to be reunited with Gonzalez, who with a warm smile led us away from the slopes to teach us properly the basic techniques of downhill skiing. Most of the manoeuvres were not too difficult to get the hang of, except for the skiing 'body position', which seemed to be totally beyond my ability to comprehend.

Gonzalez explained that the best way to adapt to it, was to imagine that you have just been punched in the stomach, and are on the point of trying to get back up again. To illustrate this point, he proceeded to suddenly punch me in the stomach. So with this kind of tuition I soon got the hang of it. After practising for a while we went back to the ski slope areas, and spent the rest of the day refining and honing our techniques.

To begin with there weren't all that many other people about, but by eleven o'clock quite a few civilian skiers started turning up. It made me really appreciate the course that I was on. The public would have paid quite a sum of money just to use the slope for a day without instruction or transportation, and that's on top of the hundreds they'd already paid for their equipment. For us the whole course was practically free, just a minimal amount to cover our food and the fuel for the truck and Jeep.

For lunch we sat about for a bit in the snow drinking coffee and eating. I took the opportunity to question Gonzalez as to whether I was the first foreigner on the course. He said that no, he remembered training two Brazilians three to four years previously, and that they had hardly understood the language either. But from this I took heart for the fact that I was probably the first gringo, and a civilian one at that, on the course.

In the afternoon more and more members of the public arrived, and quite a queue began to form for the motorised wire that we used to pull ourselves back up to the top of the slope. It was at this point that I noticed quite a lot of people looking at me. In fact when I looked around, it seemed that everybody in the vicinity was staring at me.

They could only have been wondering why this one Chilean soldier was unusually tall, bespectacled, white, and spoke rather bad pigeon Spanish. To further add to their confusion I spent much of the rest of the day pottering about and humming awful Latin American pop songs.

At one point when I reached the top of the ski slope there was a small army reception committee waiting for me. It was made up of several characters that I hadn't seen before, including a tall, tanned man adorned with a pair of expensive looking reflective shades. He stood with an authoritative posture and was accompanied by the commando Pizanni, who now glared at me from over the man's shoulder.

"Hi" said the guy in the shades. I replied *"erm, hola"* slightly nervously, as I felt unsure as to why I was suddenly receiving all this unexpected attention.

"Where are you from?" he asked in very good English with a slight American accent.

"Soy de Inglattera...".

"Speak English" was his blunt reply.

"Um from England" I affirmed, still slightly confused.

When the introductions were over with, he proceeded to explain that he had been in the UK for six months training with the RAF down at Brize Norton, and evidently had loved every minute of it. He had also spent time in Aldershot with the Parachute Regiment.

"I've also trained quite a bit with the US army" he said, *"but you Brits are much better"*.

"That's what I like to hear" I said grinning with national pride.

"Yeah, they've got loads of money and some incredible equipment, but I found that the British Soldiers were definitely better trained".

We chatted for a bit more and he invited me over to the regiment in Temuco where he was based.

"So, I just turn up at the regiment?" I asked.

"Sure, it's the only one in town".

I gave him my name and he replied with his; *"Hernan, Tieniente Coronel Hernan Faldez"*. He said that it was nice meeting me, then as I turned to leave the black-hatted Pizanni suddenly spoke up directly to me for the first time since I had met him. To my great surprise he spoke in English;

"Yeah, move your fuckeen arse!!" I gave a surprised laugh to which he responded:

"Fuckkeeeen spectackuhlar!!"

It seemed that the Coronel was not the only Chilean solder present who had picked up a bit of English abroad.

As the day went on my skiing steadily improved, and the other Chileans grew progressively more bemused. At one point as I reached the bottom of a slope, an affable and slightly avuncular man called Juan Carlos, who was known by the moniker of 'El Mexicano', cupped his hands to his mouth and shouted:

"For the Queen, eh Tom!"

As the day drew to a close we embarked back onto the truck, and rumbled back down the mountain to the chorus of more raucous singing. On arriving back at the billet we found that there were even more soldiers there than before. Some of them seemed to be in the middle of a class on how to strip, clean and operate the standard Chilean assault rifle. This was evident because there were guns all over the place, all in various stages of disassembly. I hung around and watched for a bit out of curiosity, before chatting to some of the soldiers afterwards.

They were all very interested in my 'amazing' cell-phone, which was quite advanced for the time. Showing them videos on its small colour screen seemed to be akin to showing them some sort of future, alien technology! I soon realised that I could exploit this to my advantage in an 'I'll show you mine if you show me yours' sort of way. Which was how I ended up being handed one of the soldier's rifles for a bit of a play, until the man's sergeant walked in. The look of alarm that crossed his face ensured that I gave the weapon back very rapidly.

Luckily the sergeant seemed either not to notice, or not particularly to care. We then spent the remainder of the night eating, and preparing for the next day. This time our preparations had added importance, as we would be spending the following night sleeping out in the mountains.

Morning came around and we walked towards the camp as the sun made its way tentatively over the eastern horizon. Each one of us was heavily laden with skis, snowshoes, spades, layers of clothing, food, plastic sheeting and assorted other mountain paraphernalia. We ate a quick breakfast and climbed once again onto the tough Mercedes army tuck for our third day in the mountains. The main difference this time was to be that this night we would not be returning.

On reaching the end of the only track passable to vehicles, we marched off to an area where the soldiers had constructed an array of demonstration igloos of all shapes and sizes. They varied from a very simple pile of compacted snow with a cave hollowed out inside, to the much more advanced types which could accommodate several people in relative comfort for an extended period.

We proceeded to divide ourselves into groups of three, as this was the recommended size of team to construct and live inside a snow cave. I was together with Victor and his girlfriend Rosa, both of whom were students of Proyecto Rüpü; the project for which I worked at the university. We took a few group photos, before starting out on what was to be an hour-long hike with skis and equipment uphill. This was something that did not give me any problems, but was very hard going for a few of the girls, some of whom being rather small in stature. This resulted in us needing to stop frequently, as we had to move at the speed of the slowest person.

After about ten minutes we skied across a snow bridge that had formed over an icy mountain stream. I felt very glad that the depth of snow was sufficient to take our weight, because had it not been the ensuing plunge into the icy depths may have meant that I would not be writing this story today. That aside, we eventually arrived in a sheltered valley high in the mountains that was bare except for a small wood of thin leafless trees.

The soldiers then checked to ensure that the valley was filled deeply enough with snow; a depth of roughly three metres was needed before we set to work hacking holes into the side of the valley wall. We had begun the process of digging out our accommodation for the night. It was just past midday, and there were still five hours of daylight left remaining. So time was not something that we anticipated would be a problem.

The following five hours proved to be ones of exhausting physical labour. In fact, barely half an hour had passed before I was breathing heavily and sweating furiously. The amount of work was partly brought on by our own perfectionism, but I had never expected that digging a snow cave would be such hard graft. When I later asked one of the soldiers how long it took them to dig a snow cave, the answer was *"about twenty minutes!"*

The basic premise was as follows; dig a horizontal entrance tunnel directly into the snow, which after a while must sharply dip down and then rise again like a toilet's U-bend into a main cave area that should just be big enough for the people and equipment inside. The reason for the dip in the entrance tunnel was to create a trap for the rising warm air generated by out bodies, so that it would not able to escape to the outside.

Digging out the actual snow was not all that difficult, as it could easily be chopped into solid cubes the size of breezeblocks with our small spades, and chucked out of the way. The difficult part was removing it from the cave, as working in a very confined space meant that it took far longer to remove the snow than it did to dig it out.

One method that we tried was lining the entrance tunnel with a large plastic tarpaulin, piling the snow on top of it, then hauling it all out. This worked quite well, but all that snow weighed a hell of a lot, and yours truly landed the tough job of pulling it all out.

Once, after dragging clear a particularly heavy load that I could only just shift, I fell backwards into the snow and just lay there feeling shattered. Unfortunately, it was at this moment that one of the commandoes chose to walk past. On seeing me he laughed at my feeble state, and continued walking.

I picked myself up and got back to work. We continued to dig as the sun began to fall, and the task began to turn into a real race against time. By this stage the water had seeped through my thick gloves, and my hands had become absolutely soaking wet. But I found that if I carried on working then the blood still flowed, and they never froze up.

Another method of snow removal which I found particularly effective, was for Victor to dig out the snow-blocks from the tunnel face, and throw them down to me so that I could catch them and then hurl them out backwards between my legs. I could then throw them with such force that they left the tunnel and sailed

165

through the air, before landing on a loose heap outside. This was all well and good, except for when Victor was working at such a speed that I had to be very careful of the blocks he was enthusiastically hurling down at me.

After several near misses, and at one point only just being able to get my arm up in time to protect my head as a heavy, microwave-oven sized block smashed into me, I politely asked Victor if he would take a little more care. Having my nose broken by what was effectively a giant snowball, would hardly be a tale that would impress many folks back home. Although I was hardly any more diligent; hurling the snow breezeblocks out of the entrance tunnel so hard that any unfortunate straying into their path would surely have been brained. Though I'm sure that this would have been highly amusing for anyone watching.

We just finished working as the sun had almost set. It then took another twenty minutes to smooth down the interior roof of the cave, a necessary step to ensure that there would be no drips raining down on us during the night. We also had to ensure that the floor was smooth, as any lumps left in the surface would be compacted hard under our weight to become very uncomfortable as we slept.

One of the reasons that we had finished so far behind schedule was that we had inadvertently constructed a 'five star' snow cave. It had a long entrance tunnel with a large air trap, which was followed by a very steep rise into a 'lobby', before the main sleeping area. This frigid bedroom was itself encircled by a snow shelf for our things, and had to be extended by an extra foot to fit me in it.

The Commando called Pizanni crawled into our cave and had a good look around to ensure that everything was safe, but if he was impressed he didn't show it. He then explained to us that we should take off our wet clothes and put them between our sleeping bags and roll mats, so that out body heat would help to dry them out during the night. We were also instructed to drag our backpacks into the cave, and to use them to seal the entrance tunnel from the inside.

One slightly strange procedure was that all our skis and snowshoes needed to be stuck upright into the snow, either side of the start of the entrance tunnel. This was because it was possible for several feet of snow to fall in one night, completely burying any evidence of us being there. But with the tips of the skis hopefully sticking up through the snow, any rescuers would have something to locate us by. He then informed us that the four soldiers would be camping in a tent in the nearby wood if there was any sort of emergency, and with that bid us goodnight.

I now just had one final task to perform before turning in. I really didn't fancy the thought of needing the loo halfway through the night, especially after being sealed into the cave in close proximity to my two friends. So I headed off through the trees in search of a quiet spot.

Upon reaching what seemed like a good place to relive myself, I had a very sudden change of plan when I realised exactly where I was. Let's just say that I don't think that the hardened mountain soldiers, would have very much appreciated being woken by a sudden downpour of yellow rain, splashing all over the roof of their rather too well camouflaged tent!

Inside the snow cave every activity took quite a lot of coordination, due to the lack of space and general inability to touch the walls or ceiling. The first task was to completely change all of our clothes, as we were all

168

soaked right through to the skin despite the Gore-Tex. This was something that now we had stopped moving would quickly become dangerous. The job was made more awkward as one of our trio was female, and the other member was her boyfriend. But taking it in turns to avert our gazes, we were all soon changed and dry.

We then set about cooking dinner, which consisted of a large soup and the hardest earned cup of coffee I had ever drank. Whilst not usually being a fan of coffee, this particular cup after a hard day marching through the mountains and hacking through the compacted snow, was like warm nectar to my lips. Before climbing into our army-issue arctic sleeping bags we lit a candle, so if it went out we would know that the oxygen in the air had run out. Though quite how we would be expected to see this when we were all sleeping, I wasn't too sure.

Pizanni had told us that we must be lined up and ready on the snowy ridge above our camp by 07:30 the next morning at all costs. The truck back to base was five kilometres away, and would leave at 08:30, not a minute later. Victor and I accordingly set our watch alarms for 05:30. Then after chatting for about an hour the other two drifted off to sleep, something that seemed impossible for me to do despite my best efforts.

I was not particularly uncomfortable, and certainly not cold inside the sleeping bag, but was just completely unable to stop thinking. This felt very strange after the lack of sleep of the previous few nights, and heavy physical exertion all day. Running through my mind all the time were thoughts of what a bizarre situation I was in, but also what a fantastic one. I felt that I was experiencing life as it was truly meant to be lived, and I promised myself not to forget the lessons that this experience was teaching me.

After lying awake for what must have been nearly all night, I was finally drifting off to sleep when I began to dream that someone was shaking me. Also the number 07:30 began to enter my head over and over again.

Seconds later I woke to the realization that someone really was shaking me; Victor was shouting:

"Tom Tom weon it's 7:30!!!!!"

"Chuta!!!" I exclaimed automatically as panic began to set in, how the hell had we all overslept by 2hrs?

Why didn't we hear either of the alarms? In a panic we tried to get everything put away as quickly as possible, but there was so much to do it still took the best part of half an hour.

Crawling out of the entrance tunnel and punching my way through the layer of snow that had fallen overnight, I came face to face with Pizanni who was already fully prepared and on his skis.

"Que paso Tom?"

It was a question to which I could think of no answer. He didn't seem particularly annoyed, but I felt quite ashamed to be the only Gringo to take the course and to have been jointly responsible for such a basic balls-up. To add to this stress there was a bit of a snow storm blowing, which made everything twice as difficult. This applied especially to more delicate tasks, like putting on gloves and skis, and doing up buckles.

We Nordic skied as fast as we could to our rendezvous with the truck back to base. After clambering in to the back of it there was so much steam coming off us as a result of our exertions that I could barely see who was sitting opposite me. Everyone's expressions reflected a look of quiet satisfaction, tinged

171

with a note of the tiredness that was at last beginning to set in. The journey back to base was this time more subdued, and I naively assumed that today we would be taking it easy for a while.

The soldiers had other things in mind though. After a welcome breakfast back at camp, the rest of the day was given over to learning some very complicated knots and rope work techniques.

When we went outside the instruction began in earnest. We were taught how to fashion anything from a strong rigid bridge, to a harness for use in helicopter extraction. All of this was achieved using merely a few lengths of rope, a couple of carabiners, and some carefully applied brute force.

Alas it was at this point that my sense of fatigue really began to set in, making it difficult to maintain the concentration needed to understand the instructors' words. I was very impressed by what I saw, but must admit that I understood little of it. After the training it was time to head back to the billet for our final night in that quiet mountain town.

On the way back I stopped off to buy a few cans of chilled larger, as I felt some sort of celebration was in order. To my surprise nobody else seemed to share my intentions, although after passing round what little beer I had, a drink-up was proposed. The problem was where to hold it. It wasn't long before someone had the bright idea that maybe we could take a few drinks into the army base, and use one of their mess halls.

We were soon heading over to the camp via a stop off at the local off-licence. It was here that we happened upon one of the commandoes who had been instructing us throughout the week. Thinking that our plan was a good one, he gave permission for us to enter the base. So and we proceeded to purchase a selection of Pisco, whisky and beer, for which I was asked to make the princely contribution of one pound.

That single pound was to buy me one of the most bizarre nights of drinking in my life. To begin with, we all sat around a large table in the gloomily lit interior of one of the barracks' mess buildings, chatting away whilst sipping from glasses of whisky. We were soon to be joined by Pizanni, and one of the other Army instructors. They had brought with them a not insignificant amount of liquor.

173

The night drew on, and I took advantage of the relaxed atmosphere to ask Pizanni about a few subjects that I would not have dared to broach under other circumstances. It turned out that he was indeed one of the elite of Chile's soldiers, having passed the arduous and demanding Commando course, before being assigned to a commando company attached to a regular Army regiment.

In an attempt to find some common ground, I remember asking if he had ever been abroad. He answered that he had been to another South American country and the US. It was when I asked, *"whereabouts in the US?"* that I received the answer I feared; *"Fort Benning"* was his reply. Whether he saw the recognition in my eyes or not I am unsure, hopefully not as we soon changed the subject.

Fort Benning, situated in the state of Georgia had, since 1984, been home to the infamous US Army 'School of the Americas'. Whether intentionally or not, this was an institution that had an association with training torturers, assassins, death squads and despots who had meddled in Latin American affairs throughout the second half of the twentieth century. It is possible, perhaps even likely, that similar torture techniques to those used horrifically on the Chilean population under Pinochet, were disseminated in that very same institution.

Fort Benning in more recent times however was a more conventional military training facility, and it would be ludicrous to assume that everyone who trained there was some kind of evil murderer. Many of its graduates may well have been an influence for stability in their perspective regions. But this does not override the fact that it did possess a very dark history. Its very existence was a pariah to all on the left of the political spectrum, especially those in Latin America; many of whom may have gone painfully to their deaths thanks to the training that it provided to military personnel from across the region.

I am however not one to judge a person on without proper knowledge of their character. After all, an uninformed stranger may well have deep suspicions about my character, upon hearing that I am proud to have been associated with the Chilean army. So I was content to believe Pizanni and his men to be a force for good.

We continued to chat away, with me making the most of this golden opportunity to speak frankly and in detail with one of Chile's soldier elite. Unfortunately our conversation was cut short prematurely, when my new friends from the university overheard us, and began threatening to have me shot as a spy. This was all to the amusement of El Mexicano, as he gazed at me drunkenly and began to hum the James Bond 007 theme tune.

More and more drink was drunk, and the time for speeches came around. Members of our group declared what a fantastic week we had experienced, and the soldiers replied by saying how much they had enjoyed the experience, and that they were glad to have had the opportunity to show to civilians what they were really like. Not understanding 100% of what was being said, I was somewhat surprised when a sudden quiet descended, and all of the eyes in the darkened room turned expectantly to look at me. My turn to speak had evidently arrived, and having put away a fair amount of drink, I gave it my all.

All I can remember saying was what a life-changing experience it had been. I also swore my allegiance to Chile, and declared that if they were ever in trouble I would come to their aid. Quite how I could possibly aid them, to this day escapes me. But they seemed to appreciate the sentiment.

My rather overly-dramatic speech was followed by loud cheering from all. The lads opposite me then gave the international sign language for 'down your drink', which at that point was a not insubstantial amount of whiskey. I duly rose to the challenge, to the accompaniment of even more cheering. My reward was delivered by Pizanni, when he proudly upended a whole whisky bottle into my glass. In the Chilean army, they don't do things by halves.

Awaking the next day after two hours' sleep and only the vaguest of memories of the previous night, we spent the day returning our kit, debriefing, saying goodbyes and doing a lot of waiting. We were due to leave for Temuco at midday, but a sudden snowstorm had sealed us in, ensuring that our coach stood no chance of reaching us. Utterly shattered, we all just passed out in the billet, some of us made it to beds, I just lay spread-eagled on the hard wooden floor.

As the evening came and the sun began to set, the Army found us space on one of their coaches which we duly boarded. After an unexpected good-bye hug from Pizanni, we began to make our way home. I thought at this point that our adventure was over, but I had naively underestimated the Chilean appetite for partying.

As the coach hurtled its way through the night, my companions persuaded the driver to put a tape of the popular 'Cumbia' music on the stereo, and proceeded to give me a mandatory dancing lesson. This was under the condition that I kept my fleece on, and my coat tightly zipped up, as apparently by this stage I smelt worse than a Russian wrestler's jock strap. Thus arose the bizarre situation of me, sober, stinking, and painfully hungover, dancing away with Paula and the rest of the course, in the middle isle of a coach half filled with soldiers, on the way home from one of the greatest and most intensive weeks of my life.

My self-confidence had been greatly increased by my time in the mountains, through interactions with my students, and due to my increasingly fluent grasp of Castellano. I decided that the time had come to venture out from Temuco and the heartlands of the Araucania, and that I should go out and explore the rest of Chile which stretched away to the North and South.

Whilst teaching English to some of the administrators at the government environmental agency in Temuco, I had been struck by the passion with which one of the ladies spoke of her birthplace; the southern city of Valdivia. With joy spread across her smiling face she described Valdivia as being the wettest place in all of Chile, somewhere it could rain heavily at any time of the year with scant regard for the time or season.

This inclement weather seemed to do nothing to dim her passion for the place though. She continuously praised the southern city's rivers, food, beer, and most of all the warmth and friendliness of its people. So as soon as the opportunity presented itself, I boarded the first bus south out of Temuco with the intention of seeing some of the Valdivia's charms for myself.

Located two hundred kilometres to the south of Temuco, Valdivia lies in Chile's 10th region. This region is known as 'The Lakes' but it is broadly similar in geographic and demographic make-up to the Araucanian lands to the north.

The city's main defining features are its rivers, for it lies at the conflux of Rio Callecalle, Rio Cayumapu and

Rio Cruces amongst others. Situated in a perfect natural harbour, it is about twenty kilometres inland from the open sea, and is protected on all sides by hills, islands and various promontories.

My bus pulled into Valdivia's coach station late in the evening, and I wasted little time in walking the short journey downhill into town. People filled the dimly lit streets, as they milled out from their houses and apartments to enjoy the evening's social activities. Cafés and bars bustled with Chileans supping wine, smoking and chatting away enthusiastically.

Something about the place gave off the relaxed vibe of a continental European city. The Chileans that laughed and socialised all around me could just as easily been Italians enjoying an evening in Florence, or Spaniards in the bohemian old town of Barcelona.

Valdivia had little of the 'frontier' feel of many other Chilean cities, and a rich sense of culture seemed to emanate from the streets and buildings that formed the place's fabric. It seemed that my amiable Chilean student had been right about this town of her birth, for there was certainly something intangibly safe and reassuring about Valdivia's cosseting environs.

After finding a comfy hostel and sleeping deeply throughout the night, I emerged into the city the following morning feeling revitalised, and full of enthusiasm for the day's exploring. My first stop was the city's main square, which was a similar typical design to many of the other ex-colonial Spanish settlements across the continent. Lush greenery consisting of bushes and trees lined the central pathways, and benches scattered around provided resting places for a mixture of elderly people, tramps and young couples snogging.

Leaving the square behind the streets descended toward sea level, lined as they were with bars, small shops and markets. As I passed inside one such covered marketplace, I was struck by the vibrancy and colour of the interior. The area was small but cosy, and seemed to sell everything from handicrafts and clothes, to tourist nick-knacks and fruit and veg.

The glass ceiling permitted sparkling rays of light to enter from above, which filtered past the fancy ironwork of the upper balconies and settled on the brightly coloured merchandise for sale. They gave the place the pleasant but strange aura of a cross between a church and a bazaar.

After walking one more block south from the market I found myself at the real centrepiece of the city and the area for which Valdivia is most well-known; the expansive riverside wharf.

The wharf sat on the eastern bank of the river Callecalle and was the true spiritual heart of the city. As I wove my way through the scattered groups of locals and tourists, I soon found myself beside the river's edge. I stood there for a while to take in my new surroundings.

Moored against the water's edge were various vessels of different shapes and sizes. Multi levelled tourist cruise boats vied for space with more utilitarian fishing vessels, whilst occasionally larger cargo ships carrying everything from lumber to foodstuffs would also moor up alongside.

Many of these boats carried food for sale at the lively fish market, which each day took up much of the wharf's paved area. Valdivians are particularly proud of their connection to the sea and the market provides them with the freshest of fish, supplemented with molluscs and muscles of all shapes and sizes, which will have been plucked from the nearby ocean that same

182

morning. As I traipsed between the lines of stalls, enthusiastic traders reached out to me with all manner of sea creatures, many of which writhed around in their captors' hands, looking for an exposed finger or other appendage to bite or pinch, in a desperate bid to escape the chef's cooking pot.

Despite the spectacle of the marketplace, I wasn't in Valdivia on a shopping expedition, so I held onto my pesos and made my way between two fish stalls to the riverbank itself. Looking over the railings between me and the water's edge, I came suddenly face to hairy face with one of Valdivia's famous 'Wolves of the Sea'. The 'Lobos Del Mar' as is their literal Spanish name, were not wolves, but Sea-Lions as we know them in the west.

The Sea-Lions of Valdivia are known throughout Chile, for instead of living far from civilisation on remote rocky islands, they spend much of their time coexisting with humans on the city's bustling riverbank.

It would be wrong to describe them as tame, because they are still very much wild animals and could inflict significant damage to a person if they so chose. Everything about the beasts was impressive, from their expansive bulk, to the powerful stench of decomposing fish that emanated from their whisker fringed mouths. They all vied for space on the riverbank, and also on the various floating pontoons, which served as sun loungers for the grunting and snorting animals. Some of the males were truly huge, and had thick hairy manes that seemed to take on a ginger tinge as the beasts grew older.

They certainly seemed very out of place sitting there metres away from a reasonably busy urban centre. It was rather strange to see these wild and blubbery creatures from the Antarctic, sharing a space with shoppers out to get a good deal on some fruit and veg at the market.

Despite the obvious cuteness of the Sea Lions' smiling faces and round puppy dog eyes, I resisted the temptation to reach over the low railings and stroke one of them. I wouldn't have wanted to lose an arm to an over enthusiastic sea-beast. Instead I bid the 'Lobos Del Mar' goodbye, and climbed a flight of steps up to a sturdy road bridge of concrete construction, that allowed me to cross the city's great river.

After passing across to the other side I found myself on Isla Teja; an island that was home to numerous museums, old colonial buildings and the campus of the Austral university of Chile, which was my intended destination for that afternoon.

The reason that this particular university was an item on my itinerary, was that it was home to a renowned botanical garden. Many of the region's plants and trees had been torn down over centuries past, to be replaced with foreign species that were of more use to the logging industry. Some of the native specimens under threat from extinction were preserved within the grounds of the Universidad Austral Botanical Gardens.

The garden lay between the university and the river bank and was an area of beautifully lush greenery, containing plants, trees and flowers of varying colours and sizes. It was a pleasant and relaxing way to spend an afternoon. After an hour traipsing along winding footpaths I settled down on a bench beside the river, and started to munch on my lunch. As I gazed out at the surging waters of the Rio Cau Cau, a large otter poked its head up above the surface and stared at me for a while. I stayed in that tranquil spot for another hour,

185

admiring the views and watching the otter swimming back and forth along the river.

That evening I felt that I owed myself a treat. So, after locating the correct local bus, I climbed on board and began a pilgrimage to the amusingly titled Kunstmann Brewery.

Kunstmann is the name of one of Chile's finest beers, and it is a direct by-product of the extensive German immigration which took place in the region from the mid-1800s onwards. The whole area from Chiloe island in the south, up to the central wine growing regions below Santiago, is filled with many examples of elaborate Germanic styled wooden colonial houses. Many of these are little changed from the time that they were built, still retaining the ornately painted crossed wooden beams on the exterior, and furnished inside with the accoutrements of the turn of the 19th century.

After a journey around the edges of the area's estuary roads, I disembarked from the bus and stepped out into the chill drizzle of the evening. Shining out from the darkness around me was the large and remarkable building complex of the Kunstmann brewery. But to call it merely a brewery would very much underplay the impressiveness of the place.

A large restaurant and bar dominated the area. Constructed from thick wooden beams, it had a pointed roof and was lit with glowing orange light shining out from inside. The interior was furnished in a typical Bavarian style with dim but characterful lighting, functional wooden furniture and a log bar which ran the length of the warmly atmospheric dining area.

Atop the bar were several beer pumps which impressed me both with the ornateness of their decoration and grandness of their size. I took a seat at a small table near to the main bar, and picked up the colourful and tastefully designed menu.

There were around eight main different beers that the brewery was producing at the time, ranging from traditional German lagers, to the darker almost stout-like 'Kunstmann bock'. There were also honey beers, chocolate beers, beers with a hint of Weiss beer about them, and my favourite of them all; Kunstmann Torobayo, a delicious crisp bronze coloured variety that seemed to be halfway between a German larger and an English ale.

After ordering my first pint, I stared through the glass behind the bar at the brewery beyond, awaiting delivery of my schnitzel, sauerkraut and chips. I could see the beer vats stood there stoically, their contents bubbling away as the hops, barley, yeast and other additives continued on their journey from field to glass.

For no other reason that it seemed the right thing for an Englishman abroad to do, I decided that I would attempt to drink a pint of every beer on the Brewery's menu. I must have made a rather odd, and perhaps sad, sight as I sat there ordering pint after pint of Chile's finest beer, while all around sipped at their drinks as they ate polite meals with their families.

I did not care though. Apart from the lack of company I thoroughly enjoyed myself as I guzzled drink after drink, relishing the quality and taste of each one. Several hours later I staggered aboard the last bus back into town, then collapsed into my bed at the hostel, satisfied with a job well done.

The following morning I returned to Valdivia's sea-monster strewn wharf, and boarded a ship for a tour of the river estuary, coastline and outlying islands of the area.

Five hundred years ago, Valdivia had been one of the most heavily defended and impregnable sea ports in the entire world. This was largely thanks to an expansive and elaborate system of fortresses which surrounded the inner estuary of the Rio Valdivia.

As our ship floated leisurely down the green waters of the river, between islets, sandbanks and forested outcrops, I thought about the Indians, Spaniards and Chileans who over centuries past had fought bitterly over those lands. If anything, the river that I then traversed was probably quieter than during many periods of strife over the past five centuries.

The area's history as a place of human habitation goes back not hundreds, but thousands of years. In fact, it has been suggested that mankind first inhabited the region as long as 12,000 years ago, before the settlement of North America. This would have meant that the ancient Valdivians would have arrived not on foot via the Bearing Straight, but instead may have used primitive canoes to island hop their way across the vast expanse of the Pacific Ocean.

As their civilisation developed over the following millennia, the native Valdivian 'Indians' thrived in their

189

fertile surroundings. The combination of warm weather, heavy rainfall, temperate conditions, and proximity to the sea which still defines the region today, allowed the Valdivians to develop the area into a thriving agricultural zone of many tens of thousands of inhabitants.

Then the Spanish arrived.

The conquest of Chile did not go uncontested by the native peoples, in fact many fought the conquistadors bitterly back and forth for every inch of territory that they tried to gain. After some early probes into the south and some battles with native forces in the lands below what is now Peru, the Conquistador known as Pedro De Valdivia arose to the forefront of the campaign.

Pedro founded the city of Santiago in 1541, his success partly due to a policy of befriending the local people and trying to win them over. But this relationship would soon decay as the Spaniards' greed for gold and wealth led them to treat the natives harshly; more as slaves than as fellow human beings.

This maltreatment soon caused the warlike Indians to rebel, and they destroyed the whole capital city apart from its fort and the small garrison of some fifty-five soldiers. The story goes that the Indian assault was only repulsed when Pedro De Valdivia's mistress; a woman called Ines de Suarez, sized a sword and cut the heads off seven Indian chiefs that the Spanish were holding inside the fort. She then threw the gruesome objects out into the crowd of attacking Indians. Thrown into disarray by this revolting spectacle, the Indians lost the initiative and were beaten back by the suddenly inspired Spanish garrison.

Santiago would be in a constant state of strife for the following ten years, but little by little the Spanish rebuilt, solidified their gains and expanded the city. The natives never again managed to raise the province's capital to the ground.

With his foothold in Chile established, Pedro wasted little time in expanding his dominion south. He led an expedition as far down as the Bio Bio river; a formidable natural obstacle, the lands below which no conqueror would properly tame for hundreds of years.

Heading down along the coast, Pedro did manage to successfully establish several settlements in amongst the territories of the southern lands. These colonisation efforts were resisted by the Indians, Mapuche at the forefront, during an era that has become known as the Arauco War. Fighting his way down beyond the Bio Bio he established settlements in the area that I came to know as home during my own Chilean adventures. Villarica, Angol, Imperial and of course Valdivia were all towns I became very familiar with during my travels. They were all initially established by Pedro de Valdivia during this period.

His successes did not last long though, for in 1553 the Mapuche named two great leaders; known as Toqui in Mapudungun. One of these legendary men was a strong-man called Capolican, who had proved that he possessed the strength to lead by holding aloft a tree trunk for three days and nights. His deputy was a young man called Lautaro, who had spent some time serving with the Spanish colonial forces, and thus had learned of some of their weaknesses from the inside.

The Mapuches' first victory in this war was the capture of the Spanish stronghold at a place called Tucapel. The young Lautaro threw waves upon waves of his men at the fort until the garrison was overwhelmed and forced to retreat, at which point Lautaro consolidated his gains by burning the fort to the ground.

Drawn out by this threat to his nascent empire, Pedro de Valdivia sallied forth from the city of conception to the north and rode south with 40 men to subdue the uprising. Lautaro was not to be so easily defeated however, he ambushed Valdivia's party en-route and after a fierce battle eliminated them all, except for Valdivia himself and a lone priest.

In the ensuing days Valdivia was killed, and there are many gruesome and conflicting stories which describe the manner of his death. Some say he was clubbed to death, others that his heart was extracted and eaten in front of him, that his arms were cut off, roasted and eaten as he watched, and one tale says that he was forced to drink molten gold. None of these stories can be validated and it seems that no-one knows for sure what happened, but that hasn't prevented film and TV producers from using them for inspiration for characters' grisly deaths in many a blockbuster.

With Valdivia dead, killed near to the location of the city which today bears his name, the Spanish reorganised their forces and reinforced their strongholds. Lautaro led his armies north, and for the following year he battled the Spanish sporadically up the country in an attempt to seize Santiago. However, he did not meet with success, and after several crippling defeats he died in battle after the location of his camp had been betrayed to the enemy.

Sadly for the Mapuche, Lautaro's former chief; the strongman Caupolican, also met with a grim end. After battling the Spanish for several more years, Caupolican was captured after an unsuccessful attack on a fort. He was then executed by being made to sit on a sharply pointed stake and forced downwards until he was dead, whilst his wife watched helplessly.

Despite the death of their leader, the Mapuches continued to rebel, and the fight against the Spaniards continued over the following decades. The tides of war ebbed and flowed, with each side winning victories and suffering defeats as time wore on. But the Spanish would never come to completely dominate the area, and Chile maintained a reputation as a troublesome province in which few Spanish soldiers desired to serve.

In 1598, some 50 years since Pedro Valdivia's forays into Chile's south, the Mapuche managed to destroy all the Spanish settlements south of the Bio Bio river in a spectacular string of victories, Valdivia included.

Valdivia would be reconquered in 1644, but the remainder of the southern territories would stay in Mapuche hands for the following 200-300 years. It is perhaps the city's history as a place isolated from the rest of the Spanish possessions in the province of Chile, which has led to it developing into a settlement with such an independent and vibrant feel to it today.

As my ship took me further from the city, I watched with fascination the vessels passing the other way. They carried everything from heaving loads of wooden logs, to small groups of fishermen and lone canoeists.

After a while the river channel opened-up into a large open area that was more sea than inland waterway. I could still see land on all sides, but the shoreline to my front now seemed about four kilometres distant. We

195

continued to chug our way through the slightly choppy waters of the bay as the sun shined down with a dazzling intensity.

Before long our ship passed a large island on the port side called Isla Mancera, which we were due to stop off at later, on our return journey. Leaving the island behind, the ship cut a straight path across the open waters of the inland bay, heading directly towards the coastal village of Coral on the other side of the great cove.

Eventually we arrived at Coral's small jetty and I stepped ashore, doing my best to avoid the trinket sellers and local guides waiting like amicable vultures for tourist custom. Once I had escaped the immediate confines of the tiny marina, I was struck by the proliferation of tsunami warning signs that seemed to appear every few metres on the wall of every street.

They were large and square, with bright red detailing on a white background, and arrows pointing out the quickest route to the nearest high-ground. The signs made it clear that the authorities took the threat of tsunami very seriously, and indeed the lessons of history tell us that they are right to do so. Where I was then stood, was as close as it is reasonably possible to get to the site of the most powerful earthquake to strike the Earth in recorded human history.

It was the same earthquake in 1960 that had obliterated Puerto Saavedra and created a new inland sea. The epicentre was just off the coast of where I then stood; just a few kilometres away from Coral village.

The earthquake and subsequent tsunami had smashed Valdivia with a force more powerful than a nuclear weapon. As well as flattening the city and surrounding villages, it had fundamentally altered the geographic make-up of the landscape. Rivers had been diverted, land levels had fallen and become swamps, there were landslides, floods and the spontaneous eruptions of volcanoes. Such was the power of the subterranean forces which were unleashed.

With this knowledge in the back of my mind, I couldn't help but feel a slight sense of trepidation as I lingered at that point where such tremendous natural forces had, without warning, been so spontaneously released.

Trudging along a narrow roadway uphill, I walked in the direction of the cliff top fort of Castillio de

197

Sebastian de la Cruz. Despite the extreme unlikelihood of any geological event occurring during the time of my visit, I still felt a distinct sense of relief when I had left sea level and the threat of tsunami well behind me.

After passing through the stone archway which formed the castle's entrance, I strolled along the battlements in the sun, examining the rusting remains of several cannons and admiring the beautiful view of the sea which shimmered down below.

The tranquillity was interrupted when over the noise of the waves and sea birds, I began to hear on the wind the steady beating of a timber drum. The sound grew louder and louder until through the gates of the fort marched a large procession of Chileans, who appeared to be in fancy dress. I watched from high up on the battlements as below me the Chileans separated themselves into two roughly equal groups, and then arrayed themselves against each other.

The drums, muskets, swords and Napoleonic era uniforms indicated that I was about to witness a battle re-enactment. I soon realised that the battle was to be the capture of Valdivia from the Spanish by the Chilean republic in 1820.

The war of independence against royalist Spain had left Chile as an independent republic since 1818, thanks to the efforts of the national hero; the Irish born Bernardo O'Higgins. He was ably assisted by another key figure; Jose de San Martin, the man who had liberated Argentina two years previously.

The newly independent Chile was not the country that we know today. Much of the land was still in the hands of the native peoples, the Mapuche foremost amongst them. The far south was the sole domain of small native tribes, who lived in the same primitive manner that they had for many thousands of years untroubled by the events of the wider world. Most importantly Spain, itself freshly liberated from the French by the peninsular army of Lord Wellington, still possessed enclaves in the south of the country, and was in no mood to give them up without a fight. Valdivia at the time was by far the largest and most heavily fortified of these royalist Spanish settlements within republican Chile.

Fortunately for the Chileans help was at hand in the unlikely form of a roguish, daring and ingenious Scotsman; a naval hero and wily adventurer by the name of Thomas Cochrane.

Cochrane had been born in 1775 into an aristocratic family from South Lanarkshire, Scotland. Once he had come of age he began his career in the Royal Navy, quickly making a name for himself as both a troublemaker and rebel. It wasn't long before Cochrane turned these traits to his and the nation's advantage in a sting of daring exploits. Most of these seemed to involve him showing a complete disregard for the rules, norms and graces of conventional naval warfare.

One of his favourite tricks was to fly a false flag to get as close as possible to enemy vessels before attacking. In 1801 he had used this technique to capture a large thirty-two-gun Spanish frigate using only a small sloop less than half of his target's size, and with only fifty-four crew members to the Spanish's three hundred and nineteen. Cochrane then went on to destroy or render useless fifty-three French ships during the next twelve months of intense naval warfare.

Cochrane spent the following years fighting the French on land and sea all over the Mediterranean. During this time he built up a repertoire of military achievements which were so outlandish, that today they read as if they must be a work of fiction.

After the Navy he entered parliament. But despite being popular with the public, he made powerful enemies amongst his colleagues, alienating contemporaries in the government and in the Admiralty due to outspoken allegations that he made against the Navy. Things then went from bad to worse when he was falsely implicated in a stock exchange fraud, that led to him leaving the UK in disgrace. Taking his wife with him, Cochrane arrived on the shores of revolutionary Chile late in 1818.

Bernado O'Higgins immediately recognised the man's obvious talents, gave Cochrane the rank of Vice Admiral, and made him the head of the nascent Chilean Navy.

After an unsuccessful attempt to seize a mighty Spanish fortress in Peru, Cochrane turned his sights towards the last Spanish royalist stronghold on mainland Chile; the heavily defended southern port city of Valdivia.

Stronghold is a very apt description for the Valdivia of the time. To reach the city from land was impossible due to it being surrounded by hostile natives and unwelcoming terrain. To attack from the sea was

201

arguably just as bad. The estuary was defended by a mixture of at least ten different fortresses and gun batteries. It was garrisoned by 1500 regular Spanish military, which included the famous Cantabrian Regiment, and contained a total of 118 canons.

Any attacker would have to fight through all of this just to reach the city, which itself was also well fortified and garrisoned.

As I stood there inside the battlements of Sebastian de la Cruz, whilst being bathed in the afternoon sun, I listened to the rattle of musketry and the clashes of swords coming from the re-enactors as they battled it out down below. I could see with my own eyes many of the obstacles that would have confronted Cochrane almost two hundred years ago. The fortress in which I stood must have filled any would be attacker with anxious trepidation.

The fort's seaward walls sat at the top of high cliffs that seemed unscalable to anyone without modern professional climbing equipment. Even if attacking from the landward side, any enemy approaching would surely have been torn apart by the many well-sited cannons. Around the bay I could see the remains of the other forts and gun positions. They were similarly well defended, and in excellent positions to repel a seaward assault

Against these obstacles Cochrane had a mere two hundred and fifty men[1], three small and obsolete ships, and almost no gunpowder for his men's muskets due to the partial sinking that one of his vessels had suffered en-route.

But the mere triviality of a task being impossible, did nothing to dissuade a man such as Cochrane. This was a man whom the Spanish knew by the appellation of 'The Devil' for very good reason.

On the 3rd February 1820, Cochrane arrived on the scene with his ramshackle flotilla. Flying Spanish flags from his ships, his plan was to sail brazenly up to the guns of Fort Inglés, before disembarking his men and assaulting from land.

---

[1] The Chilean government had refused to send more because they deemed his mission to be suicidal.

Inglés was the outermost of all the defences in the Valdivian region. It was situated right on the Pacific coast, on the other side of the large promontory of land that separated Coral bay from the open sea. Well sited and garrisoned, it had excellent fields of view both up and down the coast. It was quite capable of shredding single-handedly any invaders, before they even got near to the layered defences further inland.

But despite trying to use one of his Spanish speaking officers to bluff that they were part of a Spanish expedition, that had been battered and separated when rounding Cape Horn, things rapidly began to go wrong.

Unconvinced by his deception, the Spaniards' suspicions were confirmed when a strong gust of wind blew Cochrane's flagship aside, allowing the garrison to catch sight of the row-boats full of marines that he had being trying to hide behind his biggest vessel.

Immediately the Spanish opened up with all of the fort's cannons, raking ships and boats alike with devastating close-range fire. In that desperate situation it was every man for himself. Cochrane and his men rowed for all they were worth towards the shoreline, whilst cannon and musket fire lashed at the boats and men.

Somehow most of the raiders managed to reach the shore unscathed. They bayoneted their way through the defenders on the beach and split into two groups. One attacked from the front, creating as much noise and drama as they were able, while the other snuck around to the back in the darkness, and charged over the fortresses' walls.

Muskets banged, blades scraped into flesh and men screamed. Charging out of the darkness, Cochrane's men attacked with a ferocity born out of sheer desperation. The Spanish tried bravely to resist, firing volley after ragged volley of musketry into the mist and smoke, all the while screaming orders to rally round and protect their vulnerable flanks.

But being attacked from two directions in the dark, by ferocious rebels under the command of an infamous 'Devil', caused panic to set in amongst the defenders. The panic soon turned into a rout, and the Spanish fled over the walls of the fort, and along the cliff-top towards the safety of the next fort in the line; Fort Carlos.

What followed was a remarkable domino-like chain of events. The Chilean attackers intermingled with the fleeing Spanish, and poured into Fort Carlos through the gates, which had been opened to allow in the refugees from Inglés. In a frenzy of bludgeoning and bayoneting, Cochrane's force had soon captured Carlos as well, but the night's events were still far from over.

Overwhelmed by the ferocity and speed of the attack, the defenders fled from Carlos, and the Chileans once again gave chase. The next fort in line was taken in the same manner as the others. It was by then late into the night, and the small band of raiders had managed to over-run three well defended fortresses, in little more time that it took to run between them. By now a large crowd of fleeing Spanish, with a much smaller number of Cochrane's raiders spread amongst them, were all headed for Sebastian de la Cruz. This was the castle in which I stood watching the battle re-enactors recreating the very events that I now describe.

Shaken by the deaths of over 100 of their men and the loss of three major forts, the Spanish put up a brief fight at Sebastian de la Cruz before surrendering. Much of the garrison fled for their lives across the bay in whatever small boats they could find.

When the sun rose the following morning, Cochrane possessed all of the forts on the western side of the bay. But there remained more than enough manned defences between his force and the city, for his expedition to yet meet with failure. However, despite their battered and barely seaworthy condition, the sight of Cochrane's three ships entering the bay stoked the fear in the hearts of the Spanish defenders in their remaining strongholds across the bay.

After firing at Cochrane's ships with an ineffective cannonade from Fort Niebla, all of the estuary's remaining defenders decided that discretion was the better part of valour, and either surrendered or retreated towards Valdivia city itself. With news of the Devil and his men close on their heels, the city Governor fled. So, on the 6th February 1820, the most heavily defended port of South America, and Spain's last significant imperial possession in Chile, surrendered to Admiral Thomas Cochrane.

The re-enactment petered to a stop on the fort's green parade ground, with those in Chilean revolutionary uniform standing victorious over the ones in Spanish colours. Now that the 'battle' was over I was approached by two of the young actors who seemed to be no older than about 14 or 15. After a brief introduction, one of them inexplicably handed me a hangman's noose, and bid me to put it over the head of his friend.

As the boy kneeled sullenly in front of me in the manner of someone about to be executed, I held the end of the noose and smiled awkwardly, unsure as to exactly what was going on, as the other boy took my camera and framed up a shot.

For this reason I now possess a photo of myself stood in t-shirt and jeans with my back to Coral Bay, smiling as I hang by the neck a 14-year-old boy. I just hope that it was just an innocent case of doing a tourist a favour, instead of some nefarious scheme to portray me as some sort of child murdering fiend!

Once I was finished at Sebastian de la Cruz I visited the island of Mancera, walking about the crumbling remains of its fort's battlements, and crawling around in the pitch blackness of the ruin of an underground dungeon.

After that I returned to Valdivia where I would be spending one last night, before journeying onwards into wider Chile. That night I dreamed of all that made Valdivia fascinating to me; Sea monsters, Earthquakes, verdant greenery, friendly people, scrumptious beer and a fearsome Scottish sea-devil by the name of Lord Thomas Cochrane!

The riot police rudely interrupting one of my classes

The military junta shortly after deposing the socialist Allende government

Victor's team summiting a ridge accompanied by a rather special cloud formation

Concentrating on making our way uphill through difficult and steep terrain

Team photo, I'm back row, third from right

Racing to catch the end of an Atacaman sunset

A long way down...

Battle lines drawn: masked protestors and police face off outside my university after sunset

Molotov cocktails explode against police vehicles as the battle continues throughout the night

Looking out over the stunning beauty of the Araucanian countryside

Chilean 'Huasos' celebrate Independence Day in Temuco

A spectacularly icy vista deep in Tierra del Fuego

The northern tip of 'Valle Frances'

213

Death manifested

In the Navarino's Teeth mountains of the far south

Team Navarino: Gabriel Mirko, Felipe, and Me in the restaurant of 'El Maestro'

Motorcycle cops wait in the rain for trouble to start

The sun shining down over central Temuco

Volcan Llaima pokes its head up above downtow n Temuco

On an expedition with the UFRO mountaineering club

Magellan Penguins in their 'almost' natural habitat

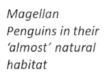

The central massif of the Torres Del Paine national park

A mountain lake deep in Navarino Island

Navigating our way past a giant beaver dam

The Jurassic terrain of Navarino Island

Land of Fire

Sat in the departure lounge of Temuco's tiny airport, I was already beginning to feel like a tourist again. This was not a sensation that I particularly relished. It turned out that the plane I was due to take south to Punta Arenas was broken. I could see it out the window, but the flaps normally covering the engines had been taken off, and a lot of people in boiler suits were standing about, stroking their collective chins and tutting. A replacement aircraft was flown in, but that too also inexplicably broke down. So I was sat in the small, overpriced airport cafe, eavesdropping on a conversation amongst three gringo travellers seated at a nearby table.

It soon became apparent that two of them were Belgian men in their late twenties; Xavier and Leon. The third was an English woman called Sally, who had just finished working in the states for a few years, doing something related to the fashion industry. They were pleasant enough company, and the Belgians regaled me with several amusing anecdotes. One of which involved them roaming through northern Chile in a jeep, driving straight through an anti-drugs police checkpoint and continuing into the desert, smiling and waving gormlessly at the enraged officers that they had left in their wake. Hours later our aircraft was finally repaired and deemed airworthy enough for us to begin our journey south. It was late into the night as we took off and flew down over the lower half of Chile's southern regions. The thick darkness of the night sky obscured any views of the spectacular scenery of the world's wildest lands, which lurked thousands of metres below.

Eventually I stepped out of the plane and into the biting cold of the Patagonian wind. I was on the apron of the Presidente Carlos Ibáñez International Airport, at the outskirts of the Magellan capital of Punta Arenas.

Shrouded in darkness, the small airport was battered by frequent gusts of air, that penetrated clothing with ease and caressed the skin with an icy touch. Not wanting to linger in that bleak place for any longer than necessary, I jumped into a taxi with Sally, and we headed into town to look for a place to stay for what was left of the night.

It didn't take us long to reach the outskirts of Punta Arenas, and before long we arrived at a dilapidated 'Hospedaje' which had been recommended to us by the taxi driver. It was now pouring down with rain and well past midnight, and the streets were dark and quiet. Walking up to the entrance of the building in the dead of night, I knocked tentatively on the damp planking of the wooden door.

There was no answer, so I knocked again, louder this time. After hearing faint rustling and banging sounds from inside, eventually the door was pulled open by a bleary eyed old lady in a worn-out dressing gown. I apologised profusely for the lateness of the hour and asked if it would be possible to stay the night. She looked us up and down, and must have felt some pity, because she reluctantly beckoned us inside.

After a fitful night's sleep, I offered my sincere thanks once again to the hospedaje proprietor, and bid my farewell to Sally. She was to remain in Punta Arenas, whilst I headed straight to Puerto Natales and onwards to the peaks of the Torres Del Paine National Park.

I stared intently through the dust-coated windows of the battered coach, as it rattled its way along the rough outback roads of the national park. I was desperate for a glimpse of the splendid sights that surely would lie at its centre. Low clouds scudded across the grey skies, concealing the mountains beyond, and restricting my view to the light green hills and fields of close cropped grass that spread out in all directions.

The reason that the grass was kept so well in order in such a wild place soon became clear. Herds of Guanacos; relatives of the Llama and namesake of the police water-canon riot vans that I encountered so many times in Temuco, were spread out across the landscape in large numbers.

The Guanaco is a relatively large but timid animal. They have thick coats of brown hair and long necks, although not as long as those of their Llama cousins. Known to be graceful and elegant animals, they can be surprisingly quick when needed, and have been clocked at speeds of up to 56km per hour. The need for this rapid pace is down to the Guanaco's main predator in the region; the Puma.

Patagonian Pumas are rare beasts and there are few people who can honestly claim to have witnessed one wild in its natural habitat. Hunting mostly at night, their wide, amber-coloured eyes are easily able to pick out targets in the bright starlight of the southern sky. The fields and hills of Tierra Del Fuego hold for them a banquet of Guanaco, who have little hope of outrunning such a beast. I stood little chance of seeing one, but nevertheless continued to gaze out at the vast landscape, in the hope of catching a glimpse of a distant feline figure.

For the time being though the more exotic beasts of South America were to elude me, and the coach rumbled to a halt at the drop off point. The first part of my journey was also to be the most relaxing, as I took a catamaran ferry across the choppy waters of Lake Pehoé. As the boat cut its way through the wavelets, I gazed out from beneath my cap at the surroundings that I would be calling home for the coming week.

The Torres Del Paine national park is an area of outstanding natural beauty, and incredible biological and geological diversity. It lies in the middle of the region known as Tierra del Fuego (Land of Fire), at the southern end of the South American continent. The park is made up of 2400 square kilometres of lakes, grassland, glaciers, rivers and forests, but it is the towering mountain peaks at its centre for which is it most well-known.

On a clear day the mountainous massif can be seen from all over the park, jutting upwards from the landscape like a jagged uprising of chipped and broken teeth. The area is frequently described as being one of the world's natural wonders for good reason. Turquoise lakes, verdant green hills, and towering granite peaks capped with a dusting of snow abound. All intermingle with multi-coloured clouds, lanced by ochre rays of sunlight, producing an astonishingly ravishing vista for the eyes and soul.

The catamaran slowed as we reached the far end of Lake Pehoé, before pulling up alongside a narrow jetty.

Leaping ashore, I made my way to the large camping area nearby, to begin my trekking adventure within the park proper.

I had set myself an ambitious itinerary for the coming five days, which was loosely based around a route known as the 'W' circuit. It was named after the shape that it makes, as it weaves its way around the southern faces of the central mountain range.

I had already used half of my first day. So I could afford no delays, and set off immediately with as fast a pace as I could manage. My goal for the day was to reach a campsite called Carpamento los Guardas, which was situated in a small woodland high above a renowned and picturesque glacier.

It didn't take long for the path to leave the lakeshore behind, and begin to wind its way up into some boulder strewn foothills. Despite being in the Chilean summer the trails were not overly busy, and I gave friendly greetings to the people of all nationalities that I met as I walked on past. As the hours went by the scenery became slightly more rugged. I climbed up between small lakes and miniature forests, occasionally crossing over rough wooden bridges that spanned chasms filled

224

with frothy waters fresh from the mountains, broiling their way outwards to the lakes beyond.

Eventually the trail turned northwards and the ground to the left fell away, opening onto an impressive vista of the still waters of Lake Grey hundreds of metres below. The path continued up and down the crests of broken foothills, all the while treading a thin line between the steep drop down to the western lake on my left, and the towering peaks to the east on my right.

After a while I noticed that lake Grey was no longer vacant, but was populated by small white iceberglets. As I continued northwards these baby icebergs grew more numerous and increased in size, many being bigger than family cars, and they were tinged on the undersides with a deep blue hue. Every so often one of them would spontaneously roll over, giving out a whooshing sound as it sprayed water up into the air.

Cresting another small summit, the source of all the icebergs suddenly revealed itself to me in all its glory. At the northern end of the lake I could now see the southern face of Glacier Grey. It was a sheer wall of ice towering many dozens of metres into the air, and stretching the entire width of the broad valley; a truly majestically sight. Grey's splendour imbued my legs

225

and shoulders with a fresh energy as I drove myself onwards, eager to get as close as possible to it before the sun set.

After a few more hours of hard slog, I eventually arrived at my destination for the day; a small wooded campsite high above the glacier's Eastern edge. Leaving most of my belongings behind, and taking just a bottle of water, I then began to run.

I ran northwards as fast as I could up the trail through the cliffs along Glacier Grey's side. Running between boulders, across fast flowing streams, through forests and down gullies, I was desperate to get as far up into the northern reaches of the park as the remaining daylight would allow. Determined to see as much of the glacier's northern reaches as I could, I threw caution to the wind as I raced against the setting sun.

After some considerable distance I came to a halt. Deciding that I had come far enough, I left the path and stood at the top of a cliff high above the glacier's thick waistline. From my solitary vantage point I could see right across the vast landscape known as the Southern Patagonian Ice Field.

It was a scene lifted straight from an alien planet. Ice stretched out for hundreds of miles into one of the most remote places on Earth. Glacier Grey immediately below me was riven with crevasses so deep that the bottoms could not be seen. This was a landscape bursting with beautiful colour. Despite its name, Glacier Grey was resplendent in every shade of white and blue in the spectrum. The crevasses' open mouths tinged with aquamarine hues, that fell into turquoises and teals as the depths took them, going deeper and deeper until the navy and midnight blues gave way to the ashen blackness of the glacier's very deepest echelons.

Grey was born from the vast ice field to the North; an enormous mass of snow and ice stretching between the mountain ranges of Chile and Argentina, and feeding multiple huge glaciers on both sides of the border. What lies beneath it is a mystery, and much of its surface is unexplored. Two active volcanoes lie in its midst, and they are some of the least summited in the world due to their inaccessibility.

Watching the sun set over that marvellous landscape I felt grateful for the privilege of being witness to such a spectacle. I returned to my camping spot with much less haste than with which I had left it, and set my tent up

227

alongside a small waterfall that fed a delicate mountain stream. That night I fell asleep to the sounds of the crashing, banging and booming of Glacier Grey, splitting and cracking as it made its way down the valley. Amongst those occasional sounds was the noise of large chucks of ice splitting off and making tremendous splashes as they fell into the waters of the lake below.

The following day was one of hard slog, as I retraced my steps and carried my heavy load around the southern face of the great mountain range known as the Paine Massif. I needed to complete two days' worth of trekking in one, so I did my best to block out the pain in my shoulders and back as I trudged onward. After a brief stop to bathe in the beautifully misty teal waters of lake Skottsburg, I crossed a long a rickety wooden suspension bridge over a fearsome river, and collapsed exhausted and in pain in a campsite at the southern end of French Valley. I was right in the heart of the park itself.

The next day it was a real pleasure to leave the weight of my pack and tent behind, and to explore on foot the upper reaches of the mountain amphitheatre known as 'French Valley'. This valley is the real centrepiece of the Torres Del Paine park. Once up into its higher reaches it takes the form of a giant bowl, ringed with a multitude of different peaks. The towering faces of Cerro Catedral and Cerro Cota rise 2000m up on the left, while ahead lie sharper spires of rock with names such as 'The Blade' and 'The Sword'. These are flanked to their right by a large but keenly angled mountain known as the Aleta de Tiburon; 'The Shark's Fin'.

As I set off the weather was pleasant, with warm sun shining on my face as I made my way northwards higher up into the valley. I followed a river which was fed by some of the miniature glaciers and snowy cornices, that dangled down from the mountaintops above. On reaching the head of the trail, it seemed to me that there remained ample opportunity to explore further; beyond the boundaries of the formally marked route.

Off to my right was the eastern rim of the mountain bowl of French Valley. The rock faces were much shallower than those to the West and North, and seemed to be quite easy to climb. So I set off with no real plan or purpose in mind, other than to see how high or far I could get, before my time and inclination ran out.

Progress was swift, and I was soon high above the valley floor. I was able to look across at some of the glaciers and rock formations, which previously had towered far above me. Continuing upwards I began to wonder at how far this course could take me. Was it possible to climb all the way over this small mountain, and arrive at the towers of rock from which the park took its name? If this was possible I would arrive at the Torres Del Paine from the reverse direction, seeing sights which would be inaccessible to the tourists travelling the regular trekking routes.

But then the weather changed.

In what seemed like an instant, the clear skies and sunshine vanished and were replaced by light rain which rapidly turned into snowfall. Within minutes the snow thickened, blowing in horizontal flurries that reduced visibility down to tens of metres. It was time to decide whether to push onwards hoping that this weather was just a temporary anomaly, or head back to the valley floor, and the safety of a well-trodden path.

The potentially perilous consequences of attempting to continue meant that it was an easy decision. Turning back, I scurried back down the mountain with as much haste as the steep and wet rock face would allow.

Trying the best I could to retrace my steps, I made my way down the slippery mountain with the weather growing ever worse by the minute, and I started to worry that I might be going far off-course. I knew that I had been continuing down the mountainside gully for too long, but had assumed that when I climbed out of it the route would be clear. But alas this was not the case. Visibility was low, due to the mist and falling snow-flakes that had arrived so suddenly. It was as if they'd been activated by some ethereal switch.

Despite being high up on the mountain, I could see little due to the weather and the curvature of the mountain itself. I knew that there was not much chance of any real danger, but the unpredictability of the mountains, especially Patagonian ones, allowed the tendrils of trepidation to begin to take root inside my chest. It was at this point that, whilst scanning around

231

for any sign of the trail, that I saw him: The Angel of Death.

Now you the reader are probably thinking that I'm being overly dramatic, that I am perhaps about to describe a difficult stretch of terrain, or maybe a fellow eccentric mountaineer who happened to be looking rather pale. But you would be wrong. Because right there in front of my very eyes I could see, clear as day, the physical embodiment of the Angle of Death himself, standing hunched right before me.

I am not by nature a particularly superstitious or religious person, but I knew what I could see with my own eyes. The figure was no more than twenty metres away and was standing beside a small pile of rocks. He was wearing a robe as black as the darkest night, and was bent over slightly, clearly staring right at me.

Within his robes I could see even deeper blackness. Whatever stood inside was either invisible, or blacker than the darkest depths of anything ever encountered by man on the physical plane. Just to clarify, lest there be any doubt in the mind of the reader; it was very black.

After the initial shock, my first thought was:

"Shit. This is it then".

But as the seconds passed by it dawned on me that I didn't yet appear to be dead, and I started to wonder when this would cease to be the case. Perhaps the sight of the Angel of Death merely signifies that you will have no further contact with humanity, to tell them of what you have witnessed. So maybe I'd have an accident further down the mountain, with the grim reaper following me down to collect his burden when the opportunity presented itself.

Unsurprisingly this train of thought, and the way that Death was staring silently and unblinkingly the whole time, (well I guessed unblinkingly, I couldn't see his face), was beginning to depress me. So, I began to rack my brains for any possible way out of the situation. Running away was probably not an option, Death I presumed could ambulate quickly, and I would probably only fall and hasten my departure from the earthly realm. The same went for fighting, I'm all up for *"we shall never surrender"*, but I shouldn't think that a skinny engineering student from West London would present death with much of a martial challenge. Then it was, with a great lump in my throat, that I remembered; Chess.

233

The stories say that Death is supposed to have a bit of a penchant for a competitive game of Chess. This may sound a bit far-fetched, but then so does the idea of actually meeting Death in the first place, yet there he was. The problem was that I stopped playing the wooden pawn and horsie game sometime during secondary school; apart from once winning a runner-up prize in some London tournament in my teens, (and I still think that I got the sympathy prize). So strangely enough my main thought whilst stood in close proximity to the Styx's fabled ferryman, was that I regretted not having taken advantage of my Father's wealth of Chess knowledge when I had the opportunity.

Now this might all read like a work of fiction, but I assure the reader that these were indeed my genuine thoughts at this time. You may laugh at this, but what sort of things do you think would run through your mind when face to face with Death incarnate?

So, with great trepidation, I made my way forwards. I hoped to give a good account of myself, but in my heart I knew that this was unlikely to be the case. I'd probably end up shuffling a few pawns about, whilst trying to get my bishops into a position to roast his

234

queen, or whatever it is that you do. But deep down I knew that this otherworldly master would be kicking the back doors in with the cavalry, and be back home for tea and medals before I'd even have the chance to offer him a draw.

Then as I edged closer, I noticed that death was pointing. He was pointing not at me but seemingly further down the mountainside, in the rough direction that I thought the base camp might lie. Was this a trick? Was he taunting me only to strike me down at the last moment? Or was he pointing to the departure point for Easy Hades, somewhere perhaps just out of view?

It was not until I was almost upon him, that I was able to tell that the Lord of Darkness was in fact, merely a very unusual rock.

Not being a geologist, I had no idea what type of rock it was, but I do know that I had never seen another like it in natural surroundings. It was very dark black in colour, and smooth as marble to the touch. Even up close, it seemed to resemble a cloaked figure with arm outstretched, pointing down the mountain. So, without any better ideas, and with the weather rapidly closing in, I decided to follow its direction.

Surely enough, a few minutes later I began to once again recognise my surroundings, and I realised that I was back on course. I was eventually able to return to the   trail, and got back to the camp without further incident. Even though it was a rock that led me back to safety and not death incarnate, I had to wonder whether it was mere coincidence the form the rock took, or whether there were any otherworldly factors involved.

The next day I wanted to push on with the aim of reaching the penultimate Torres camp-site before sunset, but it would be quite a tall order to make the distance in time. It would require me to circumnavigate the whole southeast corner of the park in a day. However, I had read of a short-cut that apparently existed which, whilst steeper, would allow me to cut off a significant part of the distance.

After another day's tough marching, I once again set up camp. This time I was on the eastern edge of the central mountain range, and close to the towers of the Torres Del Paine themselves. Rising early the following morning, I made my way through thick and clingy mist. I then clawed my way up a trail, which soon turned into a scramble over rocks and across piles of loose shale.

Drawing ever closer to the base of the towers, my hands began to numb with cold as the misty drizzle soaked through my gloves and onto the skin below.

The Torres themselves are wide granite towers of rock, which rise-up from the ground like teeth bursting out from a gum line. Their sides are sheer, and the knife edge ridges which adorn their tops stand 2500m above the ground. It must be a nerve-racking but breath-taking experience to stand atop them and gaze out over the surrounding wilderness. Such a feat has only been accomplished by a small number of highly skilled rock climbers. Those daredevil characters would have spent days getting to the top, sleeping overnight in hammocks which they have bolted directly into the rock face, dangling thousands of metres in the air.

The towers were born 13 million years ago, when hot magma rose up from our planet's depths. It became trapped amongst the surrounding geological formations, before cooling, and then solidifying into hard granite. As millennia came and went, the softer rock around these towers was gradually worn down by the powerful erosive forces of the glaciers which dominated the region. Eventually, just the hard granite towers were left behind, surrounded by the broken husks of sedimentary rocks which now decorate the surrounding mountains.

Through gaps in the clouds I gazed up at those impressive monoliths, feeling a deep sense of awe as they rose up far above, making insignificant insects of the humans far down below. To those mountains, the human race was nothing but a fleeting moment's insignificance, in a long lifetime lasting many millions of years. We were not around as a species when those mountains were born, and it is likely that they will still be standing long after we are no more.

That night I treated myself to a few beers in the campsite's small wooden bar. It was nice to relax without the weight of my pack and a tight deadline to hit for a change. There was a gas fire that was pleasantly warm, and my fellow travellers were amiable company.

I got chatting to an Australian called Chris and a Chilean called Joaquin. We mused over our various travels and shared stories of past adventures. After a while the subject of conversation turned onto the idea of going to Antarctica, something that seemed to me to be the next great personal challenge on the horizon.

Chris told me that a person could fly to the South Pole quite easily from Punta Arenas, but added that he didn't see what the point was.

"Just to say that you've been there I suppose" I postulated.

"Yeah maybe. Y'see I prefer to skip the travel and just say that I've been there, saves a lot of hassle. Nobody listens anyway."

With only one more day's worth of trekking to go, my time at the national park was coming to an end. The next destination was further south still, but it was to be one that would reunite me briefly with the comforts of human civilization.

***

For a reason that is difficult to elucidate, the windswept and isolated Magellan capital of Punta Arenas holds for me a deep level of mysticism and a real fascination. I suspect that it is due to the city's history as one of humanity's remotest frontiers. It is a past that pervades to this day. It can tangibly be felt in the air when first arriving at the austral outpost; a feat which in itself is no small achievement.

The Magellan region has a tempestuous history well befitting of the turbulent nature of its seas and wilds. The native 'Fuegians' are thought to have arrived in the area at the end of a great wave of human migration around 15,000 years ago. They would have travelled from Africa, through Asia, crossed the bearing straight and then come down through the Americas, over a period of 50,000 years. Some also may have arrived by canoe, travelling the Pacific and hopping from island to island across that vast stretch of ocean.

It was not until the 1500s that western explorers and conquistadors made their way to the south of the great American continent. To begin with, although notionally under the domain of the catholic monarchy of Spain, most of the southern tip of Latin America was unexplored, governed, or settled by Spain or any other nation.

By the mid-16th century, Spanish merchant ships were making regular transits of the area around Cape Horn. They brought trade, settlers and troops to the west coast, and returned to Spain loaded with precious artefacts and gold.

This is where the English enter the story. 'Pirates' such as Sir Francis Drake, under the blessing of Queen Elizabeth the 1st, found rich and easy pickings amongst the Spanish merchantmen. Raiding ships up and down the coastline, the English attacked and plundered many Spanish vessels, before returning to the UK laden with the gold which the Spaniards had themselves looted from the indigenous peoples of Peru.

Frustrated by this lost revenue, the Spanish decided that their best chance of clamping down on and capturing the English raiders, would be to fortify the vital transit route through the Magellan Straight.

To that end a Spaniard named Don Pedro Sarmiento de Gamboa produced an ambitious plan to colonise and fortify the Magellan region, and therefore ensure Spanish dominance of the area forevermore. He managed to convince King Philip II of Spain that he could secure the straight via the construction of two forts. One would be situated at each end of the straight, along with a series of watchtowers to give advanced warning of any approaching English ships.

To complete the blocking of the passage, a great chain comprised of wood and iron was to be constructed to cross the entire width of the waterway. Behind this would wait a flotilla of gunboats, stood by at the ready to meet any oncoming enemy.

To complete the task King Philip equipped Saramiento with an impressive task force. Twenty-three ships were stuffed to the gunwales with provisions, and weighed-down with three-thousand people. These included three Captain-Generals and six hundred veteran soldiers.

Setting sail in September 1581, the expedition immediately ran into trouble. Gale force winds battered the ships as soon as they left the safety of their harbour. These winds built up into a fearsome storm that relentlessly attacked the fleet until it was forced to return to whence it came, at a loss of several vessels and eight hundred lives!

Not to be put off by a minor setback, Saramiento repaired and reequipped his squadron, before setting sail once again. It was an expedition which would come to be known as:

"The most wretched cruise ever recorded in the annuls of navigation".

Perils which stuck the voyage on its long southward journey included: further storms which battered and sank ships, Shipworm infestations that ate through vessels' hulls, diseases that ravaged and rotted men, and bad leadership that attacked morale, and fostered desires in men's minds to mutiny or retreat homeward.

By the time the fleet had crossed the Atlantic and set off down the coastline from Rio de Janiero, they were down to sixteen vessels. Shortly afterwards one of the Captain-Generals departed, taking with him many ships, supplies and men. Further desertions occurred on the way down to Cape Horn. The result off all this was that by the time Saramiento's expedition arrived at its destination, they were down to just five ships and 500 people. Saramiento though was not to be deterred; he remained confident and determined that his quest would be a success.

It had taken them two and a half years to reach the Magellan region, but any hopes that the voyage's fates would improve from this point on would turn out to be forlorn. Storms still hammered at the expedition, and although brief landings were accomplished on the beaches of the Magellan Straight, they were always short lived, with the ships having to return to the open sea to ride out the waves and winds.

Desperate times called for desperate measures, so Saramiento decided that the only way to retain his tenuous grip on the coastline, was to run his ship aground. Not far from the entrance to the stretch at a point called Cape Virgenes, a ship called Trinidad; the largest and best equipped vessel remaining with the expedition, inflated its sails and was driven into the coast and right up the beach until it was stuck fast.

Nearby the first settlement was soon established. It was called 'Nombre de Jesús', as befitting the orthodox Catholic nature of the Spanish of the time. Looking at the area today, which is situated just inside the straight and across the border in Argentina on a thin promontory on the eastern coast, it strikes me as a rather bizarre and unsuitable place for human habitation. Exposed on all sides to the wind, it seems to offer little protection from the elements, and not much in the way of resources such as woodland, animal life or fresh water. It surely is telling that there is no settlement of any kind there today.

Nevertheless, Saramiento persevered. He blessed the area in a ritual ceremony, before laying the foundations of a church and marking out the blocks and streets of his future town. Beams and planks from the ship Trinidad were ripped-up and used to build the frames of the town's main buildings, such as the church and hospital. Such places would surely be a welcome source of respite to the inhabitants, who could only build for themselves primitive huts of mud and grass to live inside.

Apart from the stripped carcass of the Trinidad, four ships were left from the voyage which had set out from Spain as a fleet of twenty-three. These consisted of a small vessel called the Maria, and three frigates under the command of an Admiral Ribera, that continued to ride out the storms in the nearby open sea. Then one day, with no warning or even comment to Don Saramiento, Admiral Ribera turned his three ships back towards Spain and set sail, abandoning all behind him to their fates.

For Saramiento and his subjects the situation was now direr than ever. Three hundred and thirty-eight people and one small vessel were all that remained of

245

the grand expedition, which had departed Spain full of hope and promise of a new life in a fresh new land. The settlers had very few provisions, and the salty earth, brackish water and errant weather were not conducive to allowing them to prosper.

They were forced to scavenge for survival as if they were primitive cave dwellers, scratching the earth for edible berries and roots, whilst scouring the frigid coastline for shellfish. They also had little in the way of warm clothing or suitable footwear, and local Indians began to get bolder in their probes and attacks. To top it all off, winter was fast approaching.

Perhaps realising the futility of trying to sustain his current position, Saramiento took with him a hundred and fifty men, and set off westwards by both sea and land to locate a more suitable spot for human habitation.

Fifty boarded the Maria and journeyed through the Magellan Straight by sea, whilst the remaining hundred joined Don Saramiento in his march along the coast by land. They travelled with very little food and wore sandals, which disintegrated mere days into the journey, but they continued to push onwards. The going was extremely tough. What is a relatively short journey by

246

sea was an epic trek by land, and now being well into March, the warmth of the summer months was behind them[1].

Nevertheless, after fifteen days and the loss of four men killed by the native Indians, the settlers arrived at the opposite end of the straight; a place called Santa Ana Point.

Now, whilst I mentioned that even today 'Nombre de Jesús' point looks like a dire location to exist in, Santa Ana seems eminently suitable, (local climate notwithstanding). Situated at the western mouth of the straight, it has inlets, ridges and hills which would shelter men and ships from the elements. There are thick forests which would offer firewood, construction materials and a habitat for animals that could be eaten, and winding rivers that surely would be ideal for drinking water and irrigating farmland.

---

[1] With Chile being in the Southern hemisphere, January and February are the hottest months of the year.

247

Saramiento thought so too, so on the 25th March 1584 he established a settlement there, naming it Rey Don Felipe after his king. Trees were then cut, and large buildings constructed, one of the first of course being a church; the Spaniards clinging to their staunch faith in spite of their circumstances. The dwindling band of settlers managed to build a decent, if small, town with a jail, a blacksmith, hospital and a large 'royal house' fit for five hundred men, and with plenty of space for stores.

Despite the improvement in their surroundings, the colonists' grip on Tierra Del Fuego was still precarious. People were only allowed to eat every other day due to lack of food, while clothing and provisions were scarce. Rumblings of mutiny soon began amongst the populace, but they were cut short when the ringleader was exposed and summarily beheaded. The gruesome remains of his head were placed on display in the middle of the settlement, as a deterrent to all.

Having established the beginnings of a more suitable place for human settlement, Don Pedro Saramiento climbed aboard the Maria and returned to the settlement of 'Jesus' to check up on the people there. He arrived to find them in even greater peril than before, starving despite the meagre pickings of shellfish and roots, and riven with discontent and misery at their fate.

Unfortunately, before Saramiento could do anything about their plight, his ship was smashed by a storm and whisked out to sea. The storm carried him and fifty sailors northwards, away forever from the Magellan region and his long-suffering subjects.

By now, having had enough of their predicament, the two hundred people remaining in 'Nombre De Jesús' abandoned their settlement, and despite being on the cusp of Winter, marched Westwards in search of the relative comfort of 'Rey Felipe' town. Eventually they made it to their destination, but instead of a prospering and comfortable town they found that Rey Felipe had also become a desperate outpost that was barely able to sustain itself. The arrival of the two hundred settlers from 'Jesús' threatened to exhaust the town's resources and collapse it completely, leaving the town's governor, a man called Biedma, with a tough decision.

Bidema decided that the only way for Rey Felipe to survive the winter was to send two hundred people away. With a heavy heart he chose all the town's soldiers and told them that they must go back across land to the 'Jesús' settlement, and just try to survive 'anyway they could'.

A year went by, and with the winter of 1585 approaching, the people of Rey Felipe could stand no more. Under Bidema's command, they managed to construct two ships out of the surrounding trees and set sail northwards in hope of rescue. Alas even at this late hour the fates did not look kindly on those poor souls; it wasn't long before one of the ships struck the coast and was rent apart on the rocks. The survivors managed to make their way back down to Rey Felipe, where they desperately struggled their way through the harsh winter months.

By the time the summer came, the Spanish colonists at Rey Felipe numbered less than fifty. The situation was so desperate that eighteen of them (fifteen men and three women), decided to attempt the only option which seemed to remain open to them; follow in the footsteps of the 200 soldiers to 'Nombre de Jesús', and wait in hope of rescue. Nothing had been heard from the soldiers since they departed, so the settlers assumed that they must have made it to their destination and been saved, perhaps by one of the ships travelling down the Eastern coastline.

Following the soldiers' trail, they soon realised that they were walking in the footsteps of dead men, for the route was littered with the skeletons of the dammed. As the eighteen last survivors clawed themselves mile by mile towards Nombre de Jesús, they realised that of the 200 soldiers whom they had expelled from their settlement a year ago, all had perished in starving agony.

Just when all seemed utterly lost, the final few settlers somehow made it to within sight of Nombre de Jesús. Then around the headland between them and the Atlantic, they spied the sails of three tall ships. Overcome with excitement, the Spaniards used sheets to signal them from the shoreline. They were soon relieved to see a rowing boat lowered down and begin to make its way ponderously over to them.

When the rowboat reached the shore, the Spanish delight soon turned to trepidation. For their rescuers were revealed to be English sailors under the command of Thomas Cavendish; a heroic adventurer to the English, but notorious pirate to the Spanish. Despite their precarious situation, the Spanish settlers were so afraid that the English would throw them into the sea (regardless of reassurances to the contrary), that only one agreed to be taken on board. The remainder returned in the direction of Rey Felipe to inform Bidema of what had transpired.

Far from brutalising the Spanish settler who had taken the risk of coming abroad his ship, Cavendish welcomed him, and offered to repatriate all the stranded Spaniards northwards to where they would be safe and free.   However, before the settler had a chance to return to shore, the winds picked up, and carried the English ships along the length of the Magellan Straight. Before long it deposited them at the Western end, at the site of Rey Felipe and the remaining settlers.

But instead of a thriving town, the sight that greeted the English sailors was one of a charnel house. Each building contained nothing but the flaccid, emaciated corpses of its former occupants. One of which was dangling outside on some gallows; so thin that the body blew 'like a rag' with the wind.

After restocking his ships, Cavendish rounded the southern tip of the Americas and continued northwards. He went on to meet with great success attacking and raiding Spanish ships and ports, before continuing to map much of the unexplored Pacific Ocean. He later returned to England with a huge haul of plunder, and had his successes recognised by Elizabeth 1st in the form of a knighthood.

But what of the instigator of this whole sorry tale? Did Saramiento, he who was swept away by the winds, go on to prosper? Did he return to Spain, or perhaps settle in Brazil, his horrific run of ill luck finally at an end?

Alas the answer is no. After twenty days had passed (during which he wept incessantly for not being able to say goodbye to his friends and fellow settlers), and many of his shipmates had gone blind from cold and hunger, the storms carried him to all the way north Rio de Janeiro.

He tried to return to Spain to organise a rescue for his colleagues, but was shipwrecked multiple times, before being captured and held prisoner by the English under Sir Walter Raleigh, who took him back to England and presented him to Queen Elizabeth 1st.

The Queen handed him a letter, intended to foster peace between the nations of England and Spain, before sending him on his way. Unfortunately, before he reached the Spanish coast, he was again captured, this time by the French, who treated him so poorly that he reportedly became paralysed, went grey, and lost all of his teeth!

It would be a further two hundred and fifty years before another attempt would be made to colonize the region of the Magellenes, and if you look on a map today you won't see any sign of a 'Nombre de Jesús' or 'Rey Felipe' settlement. At the Western edge of the stretch you will however see a point labelled 'Puerto Hambre'. This is the only present-day evidence of the debacle of the grand expedition of 1581, and was Thomas Cavendish's parting gift to the area, when he renamed Rey Felipe something far more appropriate; Port Famine.

By the time that the year 1840 came around, the Spanish Crown's dominion over Southern America was no more. A new country now existed, born out of revolutionary conflict, and determined to exert its young authority over the length and breadth of its domains; the country was called The Republic of Chile.

The now famous liberator of the new state was a charismatic Irishman called Bernado O'Higgins. He had crossed the Andes on foot to throw the Spanish out of Santiago, realising early on the vital strategic importance of the Magellan Straight. Worried that a rival state or powerful European nation could establish a foothold in the passageway, from which it would be near impossible to remove them, O'Higgins directed that a Chilean settlement be established in the area with all possible haste.

The new Chilean president; Manuel Bulnes, then rushed together a military expedition to the area, despite there being a total lack of a functioning Navy, or even a single appropriate ship. Responsibility for the construction of a suitable vessel was left in the hands of an Englishman; a Captain John Williams, who was an experienced Navy man.

Williams oversaw the rapid construction of a thirty-ton schooner in the port of Ancud, on the isle of Chiloe. He named it Ancud after its place of birth. Once all preparations had been completed, this second expedition to colonise the Magellan region set sail for the far south.

Whereas the Spaniard Sarameinto had set out with three-thousand souls and twenty-three ships to achieve a similar objective three hundred years before, William's expedition was far more modest in its makeup.

Williams had only one ship, albeit steam powered and iron-clad, and including himself, the expedition numbered merely twenty-one men and two women.

Four months later they finally arrived[1], and stopping off at Port Famine, they laid their formal claim of Chilean sovereignty over the Strait of Magellan.

To consolidate their claim the Chileans build a fort on the spot of Saramiento's doomed settlement, christening it Fort Bulnes after Chile's first president, and in typical Chilean style they inaugurated the fortification by smashing a bottle of wine against its walls.

---

[1] It is a voyage that takes little more than three days on a modern ferry.

Four years later, in the year 1847, another ambitious Chilean, this time by the name of Colonel Jose De Los Santos Mardones, arrived at Fort Bulnes to become its new governor. Governor Mardones rapidly appraised the location of the Fort to be unsuitable for substantial further development. So, he travelled half way along the shore of the Magellan Straight, until he reached a point midway between two rivers; the Carbon and the Rio Del Mano. He proclaimed that it would be the ideal site for a town that one day would grow into a prospering city.

The place had been named Punta Arenas (Sandy Point) by yet another seafaring Englishman eighty years prior. The Commodore John Byron had rather unimaginatively named it so, when he was circumnavigating the globe in his ship; the Dolphin.

Maradones met with success, and by 1849 had managed to build the beginnings of a settlement in Punta Arenas that was home to one hundred and thirty-nine people.

A fearsomely unrelenting campaign of development and construction was undertaken from the outset. The labour was provided by the military garrison and supplemented by convicts who had been exiled to the region by the Chilean government. They worked dawn till dusk every day, with little to sustain them but alcoholic drink, and basic meals of beans.

Nevertheless, their efforts were not in vain as under their tenure streets, trails and buildings began to appear. The most substantial settlement that the Magellan Straight had yet seen, began to take shape out of the surrounding forests and plains.

The following hundred and fifty years would see Punta Arenas continue its colourful history, with numerous mutinies, gold rushes, murders, revolution and intrigue. None of these things though were enough to stunt the embryonic city's growth, and many even helped it to prosper.

All of this leads us up to the present day, where Punta Arenas is a thriving Magellenic capital. Home to 127,000 people, it is a vital port, transport and trade hub for the southern tip of the South American continent.

I was the latest explorer to arrive in this tempestuous region, and I intended to do my best to avoid the perils which had struck the previous unfortunates who had hoped to make a living in those austral climes.

With a few days to explore the city before travelling further south, I found that despite the often powerful and chilly gusts of wind, and occasional rain showers, Punta Arenas in summer could be a pleasant place to pass the time.

It was, like every other city in Chile, constructed on a grid pattern around a central square, with the streets radiating outwards down to the sea in the south, and uphill toward a large Army base to the north. The centrepiece of the main square was a huge statue of Ferdinand Magellan that sported a shiny bronze toe. It was shiny because of the many people who superstitiously touched it in the hope of good luck.

The hilly northern half of the city was a stark mixture of beauty and ugliness. The streets below the barracks were full of dingy looking brothels and dangerous bars, whilst not too far away were pleasant residential streets of colonial houses, resplendent with beautiful displays of the purple and plink flowers that were so plentiful in that region.

Down by the coast were an assortment of industrial buildings and warehouses, intermingled with rather more delightful seafood restaurants that sold fish and molluscs fresh from the ocean.

I walked along the seafront looking out over the choppy waters of the Magellan Straight, and pondered the plights of the many seafarers, explorers and adventurers, who had passed through that way over centuries past.

Between me and the sea lay a thin strip of frigid sand, which I followed until I arrived at the carcass of a rotting ship. Standing upright before me was the shipwreck of the Lord Lonsdale, a steel hulled British ship built with three masts, which had been launched in Bristol in 1889. All that remains today is the ship's prow and the bottom half of the hull, sticking out of the water close to the top of the beach.

Hopping from rock to wet rock I climbed to the front of the ship, then edged around through the water to its side. Hoping to spy some interesting artefact or other such curiosity, I clambered inside the carcass. Unsurprisingly I met with disappointment, finding only rusting steel plate, brackish salt water and barnacle encrusted girders.

After sampling the points of interest within the city, I decided to take a short excursion out into the countryside. The following day I booked myself aboard a trip to a penguin reserve and climbed aboard a local tour company's minibus, feeling happy to be able to leave the organisation and transportation duties to someone else for a change.

As we rattled along the outback road admiring the increasingly bizarre flora and fauna, I found it amazing that creatures could thrive in what is for most of the year such a very harsh and unforgiving landscape. The enthusiastic bus driver frequently stopped whenever his sharp eyes picked out one of the many strange beasts that lurked in the surrounding terrain. Living freely out there in the wilderness were skunks, deer-like Guanacos, peculiar but huge ostriches, and of course penguins.

Seeing such a motley assortment of creatures living relatively unbothered in close proximity to each other, set my mind whirring as to how they got there in the first place. Then I realised that, though bizarre, each creature was perfectly adapted in its own way to the

261

unforgiving habitat. From the penguins with their thick layers of fat, to the ostriches with their long legs, big tough eggs and large bodies, each animal had traits specifically adapted to this particular part of the world.

As I got to thinking that this surely could not be a coincidence, I let out a sudden chuckle. This was because I realised that another traveller in those parts must have gone through the same thought processes, albeit several hundred years previously. His resulting book; 'The Origin of the Species', caused quite a stir at the time.

The Penguin reserve proved to be far more impressive than I had expected. There were hundreds if not thousands of the creatures waddling comically to and fro in long, single file columns. Animals had never been a particular passion of mine, but I couldn't help but get excited about those odd birds that seemed quite human in their expressions and mannerisms.

The public trails criss-crossed the sanctuary, providing good accessibility to the creatures whilst avoiding the major nesting and breeding areas. In fact, if they so chose, the penguins could probably avoid the public altogether. But they seemed quite comfortable with the human intruders, possibly almost as curious about us as we were about them.

Taking hundreds of photos, I quickly managed to fill my camera's memory card, sometimes getting to within a foot or two of my bemused subjects. Of particular amusement were the scenes of fat adults standing next to their fluffy new-born young, many of whom wearing seemingly perplexed expressions.

The next morning started blustery and cold in Punta Arenas. Despite being mid-summer, the sky was a uniform grey and the air filled with sporadic drizzle. I traipsed through the vacant streets towards the offices of Aerovias DAP, a small local business that offered flights to a limited number of isolated destinations at the world's end. These included the Falkland Islands[1], Antarctica, and Cape Horn, weather permitting.

But it was to none of those places that I headed that cold January morning. My destination was to be the

---

[1] Or Islas Malvinas as they are known to many South Americans.

small naval town of Puerto Williams, situated on the northern coast of Navarino Island. As to my reasons for wanting to head to such a remote and potentially boring destination, even I wasn't one hundred percent sure.

Perhaps it was merely because, apart from scientific research bases, the island was the most southerly permanently inhabited place on the planet. Or maybe it was because its isolation might protect me from the hordes of tourists, travellers and self-absorbed hippies, that seemed to swamp the more traditional Latin American beauty spots.

Whatever my motivations were, I arrived at the Areovias DAP headquarters. My shoulders were weighed down once again with a large pack, and I was acutely aware that I was carrying far more weight than was permitted by the airline. I had heard a rumour that one could pay a fee and take more weight on board, I just hoped that this would be acceptable and the damage to my already light wallet not too substantial.

In the end it proved not to be an issue, as nobody seemed to even check how much weight I was carrying. At the airport we walked out onto the taxiway, before boarding the small twenty-seat DHC-6 Twin Otter aircraft, manufactured by the famous De Havilland aircraft company of Canada.

I had to stoop down very low to make my way along the incredibly cramped and short fuselage, then finding a vacant seat, I wedged myself tightly inside. Out through the window I could see one of the two small turbo-prop engines, that would soon be pulling us over windswept mountains and tempestuous seas to our southerly destination.

It was to be my first flight in a propeller driven aircraft, and this variant was one designed to handle short take-offs and landings from small runways. Such a function is a necessity when operating in the remote regions that DAP specialises in; many of its destinations having very short airstrips.

As we taxied towards the runway the throaty buzz of the engines, clearly audible through the aircraft's thin aluminium skin, made conversation in the cabin difficult. Looking through the open cabin doorway and into the cockpit, I saw the pilot raise his hand to the control panel, and smoothly pull back on one of the overhead levers causing the aircraft to loft its way ponderously skyward.

Never having suffered previously from travel sickness, I'd assumed that this voyage would be no different. But the constant buffeting of the aircraft, combined with the seemingly unpressurised cabin, made me feel rather queasy quite quickly. Initially I was able to look out the window, catching the occasional glimpse of the sparkling Magellan Straights far below. The sporadic gaps in the clouds would reveal tantalising glimpses of snow-capped peaks topping the rugged southern mountains.

But soon it all became too much, my temperature seemed to be rising inexorably, and continued to do so even after removing all my outer layers of clothing. The woman behind me began earnestly tapping on my shoulder as a signal that she needed my sick bag for her young son. Relinquishing it I began to think that it wouldn't be very long before I also would be seeing my breakfast again.

Looking around the cabin it became apparent that most of the other occupants felt the same way, with eyes shut and heads on knees they struggled onwards, probably in the vain hope of falling asleep. I decided to follow suit, squeezing my eyes shut and pressing my forehead firmly against the cool plastic of the window, I breathed as deeply and slowly as I was able, and continued to do so for the entire remainder of the flight.

Eventually we began to lose altitude, and the southernmost peaks of Tierra del Fuego hove into view. Minutes later came the sight of the midday sun, reflecting dazzlingly off the now calm waters of the mystical Beagle Channel. This often treacherous stretch of water was named after Charles Darwin's ship, the one that bore him through those parts on his amazing voyage of discovery, over a hundred and seventy years ago.

Dropping further still, our small aircraft began to follow the Beagle Channel, and continued to do so until I saw Puerto Williams' short runway appear in my window. The pilot proceeded to pull a tight one hundred and eighty degree turn to line himself up for the approach. Before long we were bouncing to a halt near the terminal building.

Passing through the cosy airport, I saw that it really was little more than a small room with a control tower alongside. The tiny arrivals office was crowded with adventurers, eccentrics, local people, various persons

267

associated with the military, and some who without doubt were all of the above. Once I had been processed, I made my way outside and arranged a lift into town with one of the locals for a small fee. He dropped me off at the hostel that I'd read about in a guidebook, where I had to pay an extortionate sum for a night's accommodation. If this, albeit very comfortable hostel, had been in any other part of Chile, I'm sure the price would have been about a third of what I paid; a premium fee for William's remote location.

As I settled down to sleep in the comfort of my warm hostel bed, I listened to the deep rumble of thunder from a storm outside. The rumbles and booms were accompanied by the constant hammering of rain upon my windowpane. Whilst drifting off to sleep I hoped that by morning the storm would have spent its force. I also felt a not insignificant amount of pity for any poor souls who might be unfortunate enough to be caught out in its midst.

Rising the next morning, I was pleased to see that the storm had indeed abated. After a hearty breakfast, I wandered on over to the police station to inform the authorities of my intentions for the coming week.

It appeared that Puerto Williams had but two policemen, who occupied a role more akin to that of a frontier sheriff than that of a typical beat bobby. Leaving my gear outside[1], I entered through the doorway and found myself in a single bare office. The interior was quite bland and the internal decor was sparse, except for the walls which were adorned with the proud portraits of past officers. I was not alone for long, because the officer on duty soon entered. He took his place behind the single, well-worn desk, and motioned for me to sit down.

Like many policemen in Chile he was tall, quite large in stature and wore an authoritarian uniform that was a drab olive green in colour. By his side was a revolver nestling within an aged brown leather holster. Behind his handsome and quietly confident features, lay a pair of eyes that betrayed a kindness and an open mind that seemed to be a common trait amoungst the

---

[1] I figured that someone would have to be brave or stupid to steal from directly outside a police station.

people who inhabited that remote and virtually unheard-of island.

After introducing myself I informed him of my intentions for the following five days. At that stage I was hoping to head south for a couple of days, climbing up and over the Navarino's Teeth mountains. I would then need to decide whether to follow the safer route, and continue south to Lake Windhound, or take the riskier but more adventurous option; of looping round the back of the Navarino's Teeth, before taking on the intimidating and dangerous Virginia Pass.

The officer's eyebrows rose slightly as he asked if I intended to do that all by myself. I answered yes but said that it was highly unlikely that I'd take the second option. Even with my sense of adventure, I had to concede that the full Navarino's Teeth circuit was probably too dangerous for me to do alone. Especially without access to medical aid, and with no method of contacting the outside world for assistance.

That said, I didn't want to totally exclude the possibility, so informing the officer was a sensible thing to do. He entered my details into a logbook, and thankfully did not retain my passport. I felt a sense of relief, as I was half expecting him to deny me permission to go ahead alone into a region where it is quite common to travel for many days without seeing another living soul.

Once the formalities were over with, he complimented me on my good Spanish, and asked how I was able to speak it so fluently. Explaining that I had been working in Chile for around ten months, I felt happy to be able to reveal that I wasn't just a typical tourist. He became noticeably more interested when I mentioned the city of Temuco. This was something that often happened, but usually because people had either never heard of it, or they had, but wondered what on earth I was doing living there.

But instead, the officer revealed to me that before Navarino, he was for many years a Carabiñero in Temuco. It seemed a little strange that I had something in common with such a man, and I wondered what had brought him to live in that far off place so isolated from his home-town.

With that thought he bid me farewell and good luck. Once back outside I shouldered my pack, took out the first page of my map, and made my way through the quiet streets of Puerto Williams to begin the first stage of my journey.

Due to my consistently dire financial situation, I had passed my time in Chile with no travel, medical or accident insurance whatsoever, and this trip was to be no exception. Whilst this may seem incredibly reckless to the reader, I hold the belief that a life of avoiding all possible risk, can often result in barely a life at all. However, a lunatic mindset will only get you so far, and I didn't want to travel alone into the world's southernmost mountain range without any sort of backup at all.

The form of backup that I chose was rather unorthodox, but I had no doubt that if I needed to call on it, it would have proven more than adequate. Whilst in Chile my father would regularly send me extracts from the previous months' British daily newspapers, stuff that he thought I might find 'interesting'.

These were taken from a rather wide range of subject matter, and it was often a game in itself trying to guess which article on a page was intended to catch my eye. In every package there were usually three or four obituaries from the Daily Telegraph, more often than not of great characters from the Second World War. One that caught my attention was of Sergeant K D 'Tex' Banwell, which began as follows:

"Sergeant K D 'Tex' Banwell, who has died aged 81, in the course of a busy life officially impersonated General Montgomery, served in the Long Range Desert Group and the SAS, was captured on a raid on Crete and was guarded by Max Schmeling (the former world heavyweight boxing champion), escaped, subsequently took part in the battle of Arnhem, was wounded and taken prisoner; he escaped and joined the Dutch resistance, was captured and put in front of a mock firing squad by the Gestapo, was imprisoned in Auschwitz, and, after being liberated weighing less than half his normal weight, parachuted out of aircraft more than 1,000 times "for fun".

His obituary was accompanied by a black and white photo of the great man himself, chest bedecked in a vast array of medals, sergeant's stripes on his arm, a moustachioed top lip, and a winged parachute emblazoned beret sat squarely upon his head.

He was clearly super human in every possible definition of the word, the introduction to his obituary

273

gave only a hint to his truly extraordinary achievements. It doesn't say that he was still jumping out of planes aged 77, that he also walked the length of the British Isles with no socks on, and had once been officially declared dead before 'recovering'.

His mind-blowing achievements and obvious strength of character convinced me that anything truly was possible with enough determination. Therefore, I took his obituary with me, in a sealed cellophane bag, along with my map and some GPS coordinates. If ever things got really bad and I was considering giving up, I needed only to read the story of 'Tex' Banwell, and I would surely realise that any problems that I might be experiencing were trivial in comparison. Hopefully this would be enough to motivate me to push on to safety, despite grave physical injury or perilous mental anguish.

With hindsight I can see several flaws in this contingency plan, but like many things in life, it seemed like a sound idea at the time.

The first landmark on my route was about a mile out of town and took the form of a shrine to the Virgin Mary. These are a common sight in Chile and can often be found at the side of the road, sometimes at the site of an accident, sometimes purely as a physical representation of the builder's faith. Often, they help to safeguard more than just the souls of any passers-by. In the more arid regions bottles of water can be found within their confines, being replenished by any travellers passing through and carrying spare supplies.

This shrine was grander than most however, built as it was within a large garden of beautiful flowers, some of which being the vivid purple type that I had seen previously in Punta Arenas. The Virgin herself was life-size, and stood within a cross-topped shelter. She clutched a lively looking baby Jesus, who had both his hands raised skyward in adulation. Both Mary and her new-born child were adorned with golden crowns, and had the same pale white skin and features found on similar depictions in the western world.

I wondered briefly at the significance of the shrine's location, situated as it was midway between the island's tiny airport and the town of Puerto Williams. It was ideally placed to welcome new arrivals to the island, and to bless the onward journey of anyone departing.

Passing beyond the shrine though was a third path. It led up to the hydroelectric dam that supplied the nearby town with its electricity, before it turned into a fragile trail that went up into the jagged mountain range which formed the island's heart. It was this path that I took, passing beyond the lonely mother and child who unceasingly protected its entrance, and hopefully, any travellers passing through it.

The going was difficult even at that early stage, and I quickly began to overheat. Coming to a halt at the end of the main trail, I stopped to strip off all my outer layers of clothing and rearrange the weight distribution in my pack. I had stopped by the side of the small hydroelectric dam at the river's head which supplied Williams with some of its power. So I took a moment to catch my breath, and refill my water supplies from the feeder lake to the dam.

After emptying and repacking my backpack, I began to climb the narrow trail that wound its way steeply up through dense woodland. I was a little concerned because I seemed to feel much more tired than I thought I should; even climbing over the numerous fallen tree trunks seemed to sap my energy unduly. If I was having this trouble right at the beginning on a marked trail,

Land of Fire

what possible hope did I have when the terrain became more mountainous?

The journey for the next two hours was interspersed with several lookouts, which gave opportunities for a brief rest, offering spectacular views of Puerto Williams and the treacherous waters of the Beagle Channel far below. In the background stood the snow-speckled peaks of southern Tierra del Fuego, these particular mountains being in Argentina, on the other side of the frontier that the channel now marked.

Climbing higher still I eventually rose above the tree line, and started to become accustomed to the exertions that the trek was demanding. Perhaps it was because I had now left the claustrophobic confines of the dense forest behind, and could see more clearly the progress that I had made. Before long the tiredness had lifted altogether, and I began to enjoy myself.

At that point I was approaching the first major waypoint on the journey, the summit of Cerro Bandera (Flag Hill). Reaching that landmark was a daytrip in itself for many of the locals. The trail that I was then on was a mixture of loose mountain shale and bare rock. It was bordered by hardy shrubs that inexplicably managed to cling to their surroundings, despite the fearsome winds so characteristic of that altitude.

After a while though these too were left behind, the odd patch of moss or lichen now being the only signs of life. True to its name, a small pile of rocks topped with a ragged Chilean flag marked the summit of Cero Bandera. Satisfied that I'd made it to the highest part of the first leg, I started to plod onward to what would be the site of my first camp. It was by then mid-afternoon, but yet again trouble began to rear its head. The going was made increasingly difficult by the arrival of cold penetrating wind and constant misty rain, but the real problem came from the now totally featureless terrain.

The map and compass kept me on a reasonably accurate heading, but the poor visibility and lack of landmarks meant that I found myself stopping to take a bearing every ten metres. On that miserable plateau there was no trail whatsoever. The GPS gave me a little confidence[1], but I was loath to trust my well-being to

---

[1] This was early 2005, when GPS technology was in

coordinates copied from a guide on the Internet. Eventually though, map, compass, GPS, the lie of the land and a bucketful of intuition got me to the other end of the plateau. I headed towards the ridge-line that should lead to the first campsite.

The weather began to clear a little as I made my way along a narrow track that clung precariously to the edge of the mountainside. To my immediate left the mountain disappeared upwards, the summit obscured from view by a sheer rock wall. Whilst to my right it fell away very steeply down to the valley far below. The expansive valley was one that was likely to have been carved out by glaciers many millennia ago. It began in the wicked-looking peaks of the Navarino's Teeth mountains that I could see ahead, and continued to slope fairly steadily downward until it reached the shores of the Beagle Channel that was behind me to the north. Just visible on the valley floor was the thin white

---

its infancy and still fairly rudimentary.

line of a ferocious river that fed the small dam I had passed hours earlier.

The valley was thickly lined with a dense forest of lush green trees, large areas of which appeared to have been flattened by some unknown phenomena. The devastation appeared to be too random to have been caused by humans, and the great patches of white flattened tree trunks seemed to be in areas inaccessible to even the most determined logger. I was yet to realise that this was just a taste of the devastation that was still to come, and that man did indeed play his part in its instigation.

Rounding yet another corner of the mountainside, I was greeted by the sight of a lake which lay cocooned at the feet of the Navarino's Teeth, and which marked the spot of my first overnight camp on the journey. Despite now being in sight it was still some hours away, and as I edged my way closer, I realised that there was a faint wisp of smoke rising from the southernmost edge of the lake. To my initial dismay, I realised that the smoke was coming from what appeared to be a small campfire next to a silver domed tent.

I had begun to look forward to the idea that I would have to complete this journey completely by myself, with no probable contact with any other humans for four to five days. I realised that it would be the ultimate test of my mental determination, amongst other things. The idea that I now might have company for at least part of the way, was not necessarily a happy one. As I drew nearer I even considered setting up camp away from them. But apart from being antisocial, it would not have been practical because the strangers had set up camp in by far the best spot in the whole area.

After another hour of scrambling down the loose rock of the mountainside, I arrived at the campsite. Setting my pack down near to the other tent, I gave a cautious *"hola"* to the group of men huddled around the camp fire, and began to erect my small, one-man shelter.

One of the strangers walked over, said hello, and asked if I'd like any help putting up my tent. After I politely declined he let me get on with it, saying that we would talk when I had finished. I had my tent up and my kit squared away in no time, as this was a process I had by then practised many times. Afterwards I went over to their small fire and took a seat on one of the logs nearby.

The owners of the tent were three lads a couple of years younger than me, and they introduced themselves as; Mirko, Gabriel and Felipe. With their pale skin and good but accented English, I had assumed them to be Israelis, but to my delight I discovered that they were Chilean students from the city of Punta Arenas

Not that I particularly had anything against Israelis, but there were thousands of them in South America at any one time, the majority relaxing after a harrowing few years of national service in the military. Many a Chilean had told me that it was because they believed the site of the biblical Garden of Eden to be in Patagonia, but I had serious doubts about the credibility of the theory.

My anxiety at the prospect of having to share my adventure with other people was already rapidly dissipating. As I listened to their stories and shared their food, I began to realise that the students were the type of people I should have no problems getting along with. I soon felt delighted to be back in the company of Chileans once again.

Despite being from Punta Arenas, a city well known for its harsh conditions, they seemed to be somewhat unprepared for this expedition. Wearing trainers and jeans, they told me of the hardships they had suffered the previous day as they struggled over the same arduous route that I had just taken, but in far worse weather. They were probably not aided by the extra weight of the cans of beer that they had decided to bring along. They had somehow fought their way through the storm, probably on determination alone, and set up camp.

Soaked through to the bones, they then discovered that the only stove they had brought with them was broken, so had attempted to sleep, wet and shivering, as the storm raged outside. This was not the end of the entertainment however, as midway through the night the winds had ripped the outer cover of the tent completely off, hurling it off into the distance.

Morale must have been very low as the ill-fated trio were forced to jump from their sleeping bags, and run around in the darkness whilst being pelted by the icy touch of Antarctic rain, attempting to rescue the now drenched remains of their temporary abode. They had spent much of the night running around in their

283

underpants chasing parts of tent, whilst being blown around in the bitter, driving and freezing rain!

All of this explained why, when I met them, they were all huddled miserably round a small fire, trying their utmost to dry out their drenched clothing and equipment.

Despite the improved weather and warming fire, the trio were on the verge of quitting altogether because their gas stove had broken. I offered for them to share mine. I had brought much more gas with me than I was likely to need, but even so we'd have to severely ration ourselves if the four of us were to share one stove. They seemed to deem this too much of a risk, and instead asked if I had any sort of tool that they could borrow.

Luckily for them I managed to locate a small multi-tool buried in my pack. Felipe gratefully accepted it and got to work on the gas valve of their stove. We sat around chatting in a mixture of English and Spanish, enjoying the warmth of the fire, and sharing around our food. They were quite surprised when I told them that I was originally going to go the route alone, and at this point they still seemed to be thinking of turning around and going back to Williams.

That all changed with a shout of joy from Felipe. He had put the stove back together, turned on the gas, and with a spark from a lighter was greeted by a very welcome blue-yellow flame. We had fire, and with that the expedition was back on again, with the bonus that four of us stood a much better chance of succeeding than one or two alone.

The next day started wet and hard. After packing the camp-site away, we set off just as the rain started to fall. We began by climbing up a near vertical face to the right of a gushing waterfall. It took a long time to reach the top, because we had to kick footholds into the muddy face just to make progress.

Eventually though, the top was reached and the going got easier. By then the green shrubs, moss and grass that had decorated the slopes below us were gone, replaced with loosely broken slate in various shades of grey and brown. It was a bleak environment, broken up only by the occasional pool of ice and snow, and the island's jagged-toothed peaks now close by to the south.

Continuing to climb higher and higher, the four of us made gradual but steady progress up muddy-sloped and rocky outcrops. After an hour or two the rain began

285

to peter out, and welcome rays of warm sunlight slowly started to dry our skin and improve our temperaments.

After a particularly steep section, we suddenly emerged at the top of a ridge to be greeted by the sight of a wonderfully round lake sitting in the bowl of the mountain top. The lake was called Laguna Del Paso and it proved to be a good site for our first group photo.

We did not stop for long though, this was supposed to be one of the hardest days of the trek, and we had little time to lose. The going around the edge of the lake was extremely treacherous, with no stable footing to be found anywhere. The three Chileans struggled along midway up a sheer slope, that was absolutely covered in large fragments of rocky shale.

Their progress was slow, and the loose rocks frequently caused them to stumble and fall. I decided to take a higher route along the upper edge of the slope where the ground looked to be firmer. After a steep climb using both hands and feet, I arrived at the top and did indeed seem to make quicker progress, overtaking my colleagues who continued down below.

My small success didn't last though, as I soon reached a dead end. Despite climbing precariously across the front of an outcropping cliff face, I found that I could progress no further.

As my friends below watched, I tried to edge my way down the steep slope of shale back towards them. What began as a slow and measured manoeuvre soon turned into a rout. The ground beneath my feet gave way and I surfed the twenty meter fall downwards atop a wave of rocks, boulders and dirt. My new friends applauded my arrival, as I collapsed in a crumpled heap at their feet. They were most amused and no doubt a little relieved that they had not been hit by any of the flying boulders and dirt travelling in my wake.

Deciding to reign in my independent nature for a while, we continued as a group, and eventually made it to the far side of the mountainous bowl, leaving Laguna Del Paso behind us.

At the crest of the next ridge we were greeted by the spectacular vista of another lake within a vast pass. The pass was named after the island's central peaks; Paso Los Dientes. It was a scene from another world. The waters of the lake were dark blue and as pure as any mountain spring, whilst the steep cliffs which surrounded it, closed in on three sides and were tall and dark. Carbon black and slate grey were the dominant colours of the surrounding rock, which gave the place a foreboding atmosphere. It would have felt intimidating had I been alone.

Further off to the south, the dark rock of the foreground was contrasted by emerald green hills, shrubbery and lakes. The light blue sky was broken by sporadic clouds of white and black, which in the far distance merged with the horizon at the navy-blue band of the far Southern Ocean.

Finally, after all the journeying thus far, I had realised one of my ambitions. Just visible right on the horizon were the stubby islets of rock which made up Cape Horn, something that I had wanted to see with my own eyes since hearing about them at school as a young boy.

Delighted by our arrival at such a key point on the journey, Mirko pulled out his large manual film camera and began methodically adjusting the settings and lenses, to best capture the scene before us. His last shot was of Gabriel, who looked down the lens with a gleeful smile on his face, whilst pointing southwards towards the far horizon.

Leaving the mountains behind us for a while, the downhill walk through the pass was long but not particularly arduous. We emerged from its southern end as the day drew on into late afternoon.

The terrain that we now entered could not have been any more different from the mountainous passes from earlier. All around us lay a verdant green wasteland. Hardy bushes with thin but sturdy branches and green leaves the size of little fingernails, grew everywhere. They seemed to be one of the only species of plant life which was tough enough to survive in that windswept and inhospitable environment.

But what really took our breaths away, were the giant bones.

At least they looked like bones, for all around us were the sun-bleached white trunks of thousands upon thousands of dead trees. Strewn all around as far as the eye could see, lay the toppled trunks of these trees. It was as if 10,000 Blue Whales had been slaughtered there long ago, before rotting away and leaving just their huge bones behind.

Evidently the island had once been home to a dense and thriving forest, a forest that would have covered the area that we then passed through.

Closer examination of the stumps of those wooden cadavers, revealed to us the reason for their unmistakably sudden demise; beavers.

Each tree stump had been gnawed into a sharp point. Hundreds of teeth marks were still visible in the wood that the beavers had bitten all the way through, to topple the tree to use for building materials.

The corresponding trunk for each stump usually lay right next to it; an identical gnawed staked point bitten into its lower end. It seemed to me to be a rare example of a wasteful process in nature: The destroyed trees and the spoilt landscape that they begat offered little benefit to the local ecosystem.

Back in 1946, twenty-five pairs of Canadian beavers had been introduced into the Argentinean part of Tierra Del Fuego. The reason for this is difficult to ascertain, but what is in no doubt is that they thrived spectacularly in their new habitat. With few natural predators and a favourable environment, they spread out over Tierra Del Fuego, eventually reaching Navarino Island. By the year 2000 the twenty-five original beavers had become 62,000, and were still increasing in number. Their colonies grew in size by three to six thousand meters per year!

Evidence of beaver driven environmental catastrophe now lay all around us. Apart from the dead trunks of the extinct forest, there were numerous lakes and streams of all sizes, interspersed with swampy ground that in places put us travellers in peril of sinking without a trace.

Perhaps I am being a little unfair describing the beavers' endeavours as wasteful, for they had used much of the wood to build vast dams which were used to grow many of the lakes and ponds. The dams were so large that in places the only way to traverse this now treacherous area, was to walk along the top of them, standing sometimes two or three abreast.

Numerous beaver lodges also poked up from beneath the various lakes' waters, appearing as large domes of wood with hidden entrances below the gently rippling top of the water's surface.

As if the hazards of the area weren't already enough, it was rumoured that rabies was present among many of the wild animals of the area, beavers included.

So, whilst trying to keep thoughts about being attacked by waves upon waves of rabid beavers out of our minds, we did our best to traverse the area. Felipe led from the front, but the going was slow despite us using many of the beaver dams as impromptu elevated highways.

Eventually our relentless slogging paid off, and we began to leave the worst of the beaver Armageddon behind. Sadly there was no time to rest on our laurels, as the area that we then entered was if anything even worse.

Thick undergrowth and numerous valleys meant that we soon lost our course, and we had to resort to hacking our way through waist high bushes whilst climbing up and down steep slopes. Progress was tough, and the effort began to sap our morale, especially when the first raindrops of the day began to fall.

After hours of battering our way through undergrowth, across valleys, around swamps and beaver dammed lakes, we eventually came across firmer ground. Emerging from a gully, we were greeted with the awe-inspiring sight of the Dientes mountains themselves.

The 'Navarino's Teeth' were just as impressive up close as they were from a distance. The mountainous massif rose up in the very centre of the island, splitting apart at the top into the spiky teeth which gave the range its name.

They looked like no teeth from any animal that I had ever seen. They were more reminiscent of the spiky dentures of a piranha fish, or the fangs of an Orc or Goblin from a Hollywood fantasy film.

They gave the whole island a foreboding appearance, which added to the general atmosphere of being at the very edge of the civilised world. One couldn't help but wonder if whether after climbing up through the tops of the teeth, one would encounter a portal to hell itself!

Alas I was never to find this out, as we had now reached the southernmost point of our journey. It was then late in the evening, and with a supreme effort we had managed to compress two days' travelling into one. We were all by that point very tired, so we spread out to look for a place to camp.

Close to the side of a large lake that was replete with its own beaver lodge, I located a small clearing in the bushes on a nearby rise. We put up our tents in the now driving rain, and crawled damp into our sleeping bags soon to be overcome by the depths of sleep.

Waking up to a cold wet morning, we emerged from our tents and began to dismantle the wind battered camp-site. Foregoing a proper breakfast, we headed off as early as possible. On this day time would be of the essence. It was the day that we had been anticipating with a not insignificant amount of apprehension, for it was today that we must defeat 'La Verdad' (the truth). I'm not one hundred percent sure why my companions christened this section of the journey so, but I could make an educated guess.

La Verdad to which they had been referring was a dangerous eight hundred metre high mountain pass, which even the hardiest mountain goat would surely have balked at. It was to be the final, and greatest obstacle in our journey. Although the height itself was nothing to get particularly excited about, the extreme weather conditions and very steep approach and descent, (on the map the contours are clustered so close they

294

almost merged into one great thick line), would make it a hazardous journey that our guidebooks all agreed should only be attempted when the weather conditions were ideal. One guide said that:

"Extreme caution must be taken at the top of the pass due to extremely high wind speeds, capable of hurling you from the top of the pass and out into the glacial valley beyond".

When reading this together some days before, we all shared a laugh at the seemingly over-dramatic style. But we were soon to discover that the advice was no exaggeration.

We set off covering the same boggy, beaver-devastated terrain that had frustrated us so much the previous night. The journey was made even more difficult by a wrong turning that had us circumnavigating a large hill which was covered with a maze of fallen trees. This made progress very tough, and painfully slow.

We were all beginning to hate the beavers with a passion, and were starting to discuss the prospect of eating one on our eventual return to Puerto Williams.

295

Eventually extricating ourselves from the maze, we set eyes on what was the base of 'La Verdad'.

At this stage though it looked unimpressive; its heights were hidden behind the tree-covered foothills. We ate lunch next to a fast-flowing mountain stream. I cooked up a large meal of 'tomato sausagey pasta stuff™' that, along with some of our emergency chocolate ration, was shared amongst the group. After lunch the going got steeper, and harder to navigate, and we lost the trail for at least an hour.

Gabriel was leading keenly from the front, but I eventually felt that I had to call a halt and have a confab, as we seemed unable to locate the pass that we so desperately needed. After checking both maps and taking compass bearings, I confirmed my suspicions by turning on the GPS.

Sure enough, we were on the wrong course. We then had to spend time squeezing through trees and foliage, and up steep slopes of rocky scree, before I eventually saw the ever-welcome sight of a 'monolito' (cairn), marking the way ahead. From there the going got much tougher, as the steep incline meant that we were climbing with hands and feet up a very wet and slippery cliff face.

After a while though the terrain levelled out a bit, and we began to take our first steps into the high mountain pass. I knew at that point that we were tight for time to make the next camp location. I was also anxious because the weather seemed to be threateningly closing in. I wanted to spend as little time in the area as possible. If a storm were to brew up or the light fade, we would be dangerously exposed and probably lost, which could easily result in disastrous consequences.

My amigos however did not seem to share my sense of urgency and to my consternation lingered, taking photos of the impressive terrain. One of the first sights that had greeted us upon ascending to the plateau was the Argentinean town of Ushauia, which lies across the water on the northern shore of the Beagle Channel. At that time of day it reflected the sun towards us. The town shined intensely like a priceless, sparkling jewel, hovering, mirage-like in the distance.

I was temporarily stayed by the majesty of this vision, but rapidly approaching storm clouds to the south, were quick to remind me of where my priorities should lie. I took the lead, making my way from monolith to monolith across a featureless land carpeted by loose grey rock. I was very keen to be out of that place, as it was without doubt the most dangerous part of the expedition. Being stuck there when the light faded, and the weather came in, would surely be a recipe for calamity.

Although only eight hundred metres above sea level; an elevation which most mountaineers would scoff at, we were at that point on the highest part of the world's southernmost mountain range (Antarctica excluded), and in very close proximity to Cape Horn, with no natural shelter from the elements. I was desperate to press on with all possible haste. So I was not particularly impressed when I turned and saw my mates taking photos of each other against the 'Book of Revelations' style backdrop, seemingly oblivious to the imminent danger. One of them even commented:

"Chuta weon, estamos en Mordor!!"

Or; *"bloody hell mate, we're in Mordor!"* as we might say in English.

Deciding that the best method to get us out of there was to press on ahead and get the others to follow, I moved as fast as I could navigate. The wind increased incrementally in power, slowly at first, but rapidly building up to a potent force. Despite carrying almost half my body weight on my back, the power of the wind made me feel like I was walking on the moon. All I needed to do was propel myself upwards slightly on tip toes and the wind would launch me forwards several metres. It was quite an exhilarating experience to be able to fly such distances whilst carrying such weight, expending virtually no effort at all.

Launching ourselves forwards with large bounds, we began to make up for lost time, and before long had reached the northern edge of the mountain plateau. We were now at the point that the guide book had warned us about, and we quickly realised that it hadn't been exaggerating after all.

Fearsome winds ripped past us and over the edge of the plateau's lip, down into the valley beyond. It took every effort of our muscles and sinews just to stay upright. Sometimes we even had to hold on to each other, to prevent someone from being blown over the edge of the precipice.

One by one we lowered each other down over the edge, and footstep by precarious footstep we trod a slippery path down the steep mountainside, dislodging rocks as we went. Once at the bottom, we all let out a sigh of relief at the released tension, grateful that all four of us had got down the worst section of the route unscathed.

Once again, a large lake in a bowl of the mountainside was an obstacle in our path. We edged our way carefully around its western shore for an hour, before arriving at its northern tip. Here a waterfall took the lake's water down another rocky cliff face, before it fell into a fast-flowing stream that led off into the forest down below.

Although less strong than at the top of the ridge, the wind was still so fierce that it blew the water of the lake through the air horizontally at the top of the waterfall, out into the void of the atmosphere beyond.

As I inched over the waterfall's edge and started to climb down its slippery rock surface, I suddenly came face to face with the vacantly staring eyes of a rotting corpse.

300

The corpse was that of a large dead beaver, wedged between the water and a rock at the top of the waterfall. The body was bloated with inner decay and the face had been bleached completely white by the water and sun. It can't have been dead too long, because the eyes remained bulging slightly out of their sockets, as they looked out from the creature's lifeless face.

Shuddering with revulsion, we climbed down past the dead animal. After several metres of descent, we were relieved to find ourselves out of the worst of the wind. At the bottom of the waterfall the ground levelled out, and the stream soon became wider and deeper as rivulets from different parts of the mountain fed its flow.

Vegetation began to grow up all around us, and after a risky jump over one of the stream's narrower points, we found ourselves within a thick forest. It was now several days since I had last seen a tree that wasn't dead or bent over double from the winds, so the presence of the forest was a welcome sight.

The rain continued to fall, but we were all now protected slightly by the leafy canopy above our heads. Nevertheless, the evening was drawing in, so after trekking deeper into the forest's interior, we came across a clearing and began the process of setting-up camp for the night.

By this time we were all pretty much out of water, having filled our flasks several times to slake our thirst during the day's exertions.

So whilst the rest of the team got hard to work erecting tents and starting a fire, I retraced my steps back to the turbulent stream to top up our supplies. As I bent down to refill my canteen from the mountain stream, my mind drifted back to a piece of outdoor survival advice I had once picked up:

"When drinking water from rivers, always check half a mile upstream in case there are the dead bodies of any animals near to the water's edge."

With this thought in my head an image of the bleached, agonised face of the dead beaver flashed into my mind. The dead beaver still lay wedged barely three hundred metres upstream from the very water that I'd been drinking only moments previously. As if on cue, my stomach began to ache, and I started to feel slightly ill.

I hoped that this feeling was purely psychological, but that didn't stop me adding a double dosage of puri-tabs to the water that I'd just filled. I guzzled the resulting solution; it tasted like water from an over-chlorinated inner-city swimming pool. It seemed to 'cure' me though, and I made my way back to the tent to discover that the lads were having a hell of a time trying to get a fire going.

Despite an abundant supply of wood, fire-lighting materials and shelter from the wind, we slaved away for the best part of two hours with no result. Continuing for a while after the others had given up, I eventually admitted defeat and retreated cold and wet into the tent for some soup, the last of the jam paste and a bit of friendly banter.

Experimenting with my camera, Mirko set the shutter speed very low and took a series of atmospheric photos that, whilst slightly haunting, summed up our coldness and fatigue rather well. It wasn't long before the exertions of the day began to tell. I bid my amigos goodnight, headed for my tent, and crawled into the warm cocoon of the sleeping bag within.

I was the first to rise the following morning, unzipping my tent to a sunny and fresh southern sky. After gathering water and firewood, I renewed my attempt at fire-making, and this time was soon to be rewarded with a crackling blaze. It was as if the skills of the legendary English woodsman Ray Mears were with me that morning, and upon waking, my amigos were suitably impressed by the flames that welcomed them. This was to be the last day of our trek, and we were in no hurry to leave that tranquil spot.

After a pleasant breakfast we set off through the forest. We climbed under and over moss-covered fallen tree trunks and made our way through foliage, as the ground beneath our feet gradually sank lower and lower towards sea level.

As the morning wore on, the sky above began to clear. It was not long before the sun's warm rays filtered their way through the forest canopy, and gave our surroundings a beautiful twinkling hue.

Wild flowers and exotic shrubs soon decorated our route, and we laughed and joked as we walked. We were happy in the knowledge that we were on the final leg of this expedition. It was around midday when we stepped out from the trees into clear air, finding ourselves by the side of the road which ran along the coast to Puerto Williams.

As we trekked along the road, a friendly local woman pulled up alongside us in a car. Mirko, Gabriel and Felipe conversed with her in rapid Castellano, and it wasn't long before the lady offered us a lift into town. The four of us crammed ourselves inside her small pick-up truck, sitting practically on top of each other as we bounced our way around the coastline.

We arrived back in Puerto Williams and thanked the Señora before bidding her goodbye. We then piled into a local cantina for a well-earned beer. After reflecting with great joy upon the wonderful experience that we had all shared, and talking of how we had bonded so well and had become good friends, our thoughts turned to the subject of revenge.

Whilst struggling through the beaver devastated terrain mid-way through our journey, we had resolved that on reaching civilisation once again we would take revenge upon the sharp toothed flat tailed rodents. The best way to realise this vengeance against beaver-kind seemed to be to eat one of them. So that is how we found ourselves that same evening, sat around a circular table in William's most authentic local restaurant; El Resto Del Sur.

The restaurant had a reputation for serving eccentric dishes of unusual foods. One of the highlights of the menu was of course; beaver.

Unfortunately, even in death the beaver proved to be an annoyance; the meat was difficult to get at amongst the animal's many interwoven bones. But the meal itself was good, and was made all the better by the antics of the restaurant's eccentric chef and proprietor; Carlos Arriagada.

Dressed in a chef's hat and bright yellow cooking outfit, Carlos showed great interest in the four of us. On hearing of our adventures in the island's southern wilderness, he regaled us with his own outlandish tales. One such story was the tale of the man who lived in the first house on Navarino Island. He apparently had shipped the sizeable dwelling over flat-packed from the Argentinean port of Ushuaia. He had then lived out his days as a hermit, hidden away in the island's outer reaches, staying in his house in the forest and hunting wild bulls and condors with an assault rifle!

Our chatting and joking made the evening pass by quickly. Carlos impressed us so much with his cooking, the liberal offerings of wine and friendly conversation, that the Chileans nicknamed him *'El Maestro'*.

Upon hearing that we had yet to organise a place to stay for the night, El Maestro extended his hospitality by inviting us to stay in his home. So when nightfall came the four of us slept soundly in bunks with full bellies and contented minds, within the warm confines of Carlos' home.

Rising early the next morning, Carlos and his wife made us a hearty breakfast. We gratefully devoured this before cramming ourselves into his extremely dilapidated pick-up truck. Resplendent as it was with dents, holes and a twisted chassis, it was a miracle that the thing could move at all under its own power. Gabriel got the short straw when he sat in the passenger seat, which was soaked where the rain had been coming in through a broken window.

The reason that we were squashed together so awkwardly, was because the previous night El Maestro had revealed to us that Puerto Williams, whilst being the most southerly populated town on the planet, was not actually the most southerly settlement. The honour of that appellation fell to an unheard-of fishing village on the untamed East Coast of Navarino Island. It was called Puerto Toro, or 'Bull Port' in English.

El Maestro had a cabin there where he lived for some months of the year, and he was due to visit by ship the next day. After more than a few glasses of fine Chilean wine he had invited Mirko, Gabriel, Felipe and myself along. We hadn't hesitated to enthusiastically accept his offer.

Early the following morning El Maestro managed to do a deal with the harbour master and arrange passage for the three Chileans. But unfortunately in my case things would be more difficult. As I was quite obviously a foreigner, the official was not prepared to allow me onboard without prior agreement from the authorities, and no amount of pleading or coercion from my friends or El Maestro was able to persuade him otherwise.

Undeterred, El Maestro and the three amigos told me just to be quiet and sit in the truck. So I sat there, half nervous and half bemused, waiting to see how things would pan out.

As we approached the ferry I wondered how I was going to get on board. Everyone else was on the manifest except me. I didn't even have a ticket, and the harbour master had bluntly said that if I wasn't on the manifest then I wasn't going. But in the usual Chilean way my amigos had in a blasé fashion, told me not to worry about it and that they'd 'sort it out'.

After stopping to converse with some of his friends, Carlos drove the pick-up onto the ferry and got out to attend to some of his business. As the minutes passed by, I began to think that I'd made it, and couldn't believe how easy it had been. Then there was a knock at the window. I opened the door to be faced with a young man in Chilean naval uniform.

"Your names please" he said, looking down at the clipboard in his hands.

My stomach clenched as my friends gave their names one by one.

"Gabriel" tick,

"Mirco" tick,

"Felipe" tick. The official turned his inquisitive gaze to me.

Not knowing what to do, I did and said absolutely nothing, merely staring blankly back at him.

He stared back expectantly, perhaps wondering if I was suffering from some sort of mental retardation. I felt my willpower starting to crack and prepared to confess.

"Carlos, his name's Carlos" Felipe said suddenly.

"Carlos who?" the sailor replied as Felipe's eyes flicked down at the list,

"Carlos Arriagada" was the answer.

Looking down at the list, the sailor razed his gaze to me once more, perhaps wondering if I was deaf, dumb, mentally ill, or just very shy. After another uncomfortable pause, he looked back down, put his pen to the list, made a small tick, then turned and went away, continuing his inspection of the ship.

After a few seconds, everyone in the car released their breath.

"Bloody hell weon! You're a stowaway!" Mirco expressed what everyone else was thinking.

I couldn't believe we'd got away with it, I felt excited and at the same time uncomfortable. The

310

thought of entering the southernmost inhabited place on the planet as a stowaway was quite a thrill, but at the same time I was slightly ill at ease with the illegality of it.

We were in a very militarised area[1], that not long ago was in a territorial dispute that had almost led to war between Chile and Argentina. Also, I was a British person illegally on board a ship that was to pass very close to the Argentinean mainland, in fact it was the nearest land that Argentina has to the Falkland Islands. If caught I'd try to play the ignorant foreigner card again, but I had real doubts as to whether it would help in that part of the world.

We continued to chat for a while, but when there was a knock at the window five minutes later, and I looked out to see a rather un-amused looking Chilean Navy sailor, with Carlos alongside him, I realised that the game was up.

---

[1]Puerto Williams wasn't really much more than a naval base with a town attached.

311

Luckily though, Carlos' influence seemed to help, and the sailor merely checked my passport and noted my name down on the list. Shortly afterwards the ferry began to shake and rumble as its engines built up the revs, and it slowly pulled away from the shore and out into the cold greyness of the Beagle channel. I was on my way to Puerto Toro!

Carlos went off again to another part of the ship, while the rest of us stayed crammed like sardines in the back of his pick-up. At first, we were all quite excited, but after a few minutes the realisation dawned that our 'trip to the end of the world' was actually going to be a very boring three-hour boat journey.

Gabriel fiddled with the radio, trying his best to find a signal, but the only station worth listening to was an Argentinean one called *Radio Infinito*. It played the sort of laid back melodies that people only listen to if they really have nothing else to do. Someone found an old blanket and laid it across the three of us, and the exertions of the previous days suddenly began to tell. It wasn't long before my head lolled to one side, coming to rest on Mirko's shoulder, and the four of us fell into a deep sleep.

An hour or two later I awoke. Looking out the windows I noticed that the rain had slackened off, so we left the pick-up and went out on deck to have a look at our surroundings. People had remarked that this part of the world bears a resemblance to parts of Scotland, and there in the middle of the Beagle Channel that was certainly true. The rugged coastline of Argentinean Tierra Del Fuego was clearly visible a mile or so to the north, whilst Navarino Island lay a little closer on our starboard side. The waters around us were still and calm; something that was a great relief to Gabriel as he did not travel well.

My three friends had originally arrived at Puerto Williams by plane. Thanks to family connections they'd managed to get a very cheap ride in, on an aircraft of the Chilean Marines. Whilst this was good news for their wallets, the same certainly could not be said for their stomachs. Their description of the flight had made mine sound like a pleasure cruise by comparison. Buffeted by severe turbulence and thrown about all over the place, it had sounded horrendous. Gabriel had suffered particularly badly, and had vomited copiously as a result of the travel sickness.

The white and strained expression on Gabriel's face, made it plain for all to see that he wasn't enjoying this boat trip very much either. But he was going to somehow have to learn to cope with it, because the three amigos intended to return later to their home port of Punta Arenas by ship. That would be a journey of several days through a cluttered mixture of rugged rocky islands, mighty ice-bergs and majestic glaciers.

Apart from travel sickness, Gabriel did have good reason to be concerned; the seas through which we were then sailing were famous for being the most dangerous in the world. I remember being transfixed in primary school by stories of early explorers sailing in the seas around Cape Horn. They were tales of waves taller than the highest buildings, winds that could tear a ship apart, and of the hundreds of ships and men that fell beneath the waves, never again to return.

As we continued making our lethargic progress through Beagle's now calm waters, there was plenty of evidence to be seen of disasters past. We were up on the high deck next to the bridge when Felipe pointed out to

314

me the wreck of a large steel ship, half in, half out of the water, and rusting orangey-brown with age.

It had apparently been a floating library owned by missionaries, some of the many who had travelled there over the centuries, to bring the word of God to the inhabitants of the unforgiving landscape. God evidently had other plans for the souls on that ship though, and whether they escaped, or had sunk forever beneath the waves shall remain a mystery to me.

Eventually we rounded the north-east corner of the island before continuing steadily southwards, gradually drawing nearer to our destination. A while later after rounding one final outcrop, Puerto Toro crept into view.

Finally I was able to set my gaze upon the southernmost permanently inhabited spot on the planet. To my eyes the tiny hamlet seemed a welcoming but hardy place. Located in a small inlet on the eastern side of the island, Toro was a tiny community of fishermen and their families. They lived close together in small single-story houses made from wood and tin. The hamlet had an element of beauty to it, with wild flowers among the blades of grass, and steep rocky hills surrounding it on three sides.

We disembarked from the ferry onto the solitary weather-beaten pier, and began to explore the local environment. Our first stop was a small wooden church on the seafront. It was sparsely decorated, with none of the finery typical of many religious establishments closer to home. There was however a strange aura about the place, one that bade us four young men to fall suddenly and inexplicably silent.

On one of the walls was hung a picture of a sailor battling with the wheel of an unseen ship. The expression on his face suggested that the man was in a desperate struggle, for the life of himself and those of his shipmates. The sailor, despite being of strong build and unquestionable courage, looked to be in dire peril. Behind him stood another person. It was a person dressed in flowing robes who had laid one of his hands reassuringly on the sailor's shoulder, protecting and guiding him through the troubles ahead. That person was Jesus.

I think that the image made us all stop and fall into a quiet reverie for a moment. We thought of all the travellers over hundreds of years who had fought their way around the perilous seas of that coastline. Many of whom would have counted their final resting place as the bottom of the South Atlantic Ocean.

Leaving the church, we walked around the rest of the settlement. We visited the tiny school that taught all of seven children, and nosed around the houses and huts in which the villagers lived. The only other event happening in the tiny outpost that day, seemed to be a small party of video-camera toting German students. I understood nothing of what they were saying, but it appeared that they were filming a documentary about the odd-looking stuffed corpse of a big dead rat.

It wasn't long before we were invited to earn our passage to this remotest of places. We were asked to help to unload a season's supply of firewood into Carlos' cabin, so that he would be able to keep warm through the following winter.

One by one we took turns to haul logs from the back of a truck. The vehicle was so battered that it looked like it had been set upon by a hoard of raving sledgehammer-wielding lunatics, and then thrown down a mountain for good measure. It didn't take long for us to become covered from neck to waist in mud and dirt from the heavy logs, but I was pleased to be doing honest physical work that would be of help to someone. Once the job was finished, I felt a sense of pride that a man at the very end of the world would be warm in the winter, thanks partly to the efforts of my Chilean friends and I.

The four of us then joined Carlos inside his small cabin, and stood chatting in the gloom of the sparse interior. It seemed like a lonely place to exist, but was made warmer when Felipe managed to find an old wrought iron gas burner. He used it to brew up some coffee whilst our faces glowed with the flickering blue light of the soft flames.

When the time came to say goodbye we all embraced Carlos with a genuine feeling of familial warmth, and expressed our gratitude for his generous hospitality. Then the four of us turned and boarded the ship for the half day voyage back to Puerto Williams.

Soon the time came for me to also bid a fond farewell to my Chilean friends. In the short period that I had known them I had formed a close bond with the three amigos. In time all of them would go on to great successes; Felipe as a journalist, Mirko as a

318

photographer and artist, and Gabriel as a well-known and radical politician, who would fight relentlessly for the rights of the Magellan people and a fair education system for all.

Before departing Navarino Island myself, there was one final task that I desired to complete; to come face to face with the last of the line of pure-blooded Yaghan Indians.

The Yaghan, like their Mapuche brethren to the north, are a tribe of people native to South America. Their territory once comprised of the lands at the southern tip of Patagonia extending all the way down to Cape Horn itself, which makes them the southernmost native people known to exist on the planet.

Sadly though, throughout history they have fared even worse than the Mapuche and other native peoples. Whilst they had never been a highly populous people, they are now less than 1700 in number.

What truly amazed me was how a native people, bereft of modern clothing or any of the advancements of the outside world, could have survived for so long in such a harsh and bitterly inhospitable environment.

Throughout my time on Navarino Island the weather had been relatively mild, for it was the beginning of the Chilean Summer. So aside from the occasional rainstorm, it had been reasonably warm and comfortable at the infamous tip of the world. However, I was well aware that for most of the year things were very different. Wet, freezing, and fierce storms were more the norm than the exception.

It required no great feat of imagination to wonder at the hardiness required of a native people in order to survive in such a climate. When Charles Darwin travelled those parts of the world in 1832, he had several encounters with the native Fuegians. In his book *'The Voyage of the Beagle'* he describes them in language that today seems shocking by its bluntness[1]:

"I could not have believed how wide was the difference between savage and civilized man: it is greater than between a

---

[1] And what in modern times we would judge to be political incorrectness and probably outright racism.

wild and domesticated animal, in as much as in man there is a greater power of improvement....These Fuegians are a very different race from the stunted, miserable wretches farther westward; and they seem closely allied to the famous Patagonians of the Strait of Magellan. Their only garment consists of a mantle made of guanaco skin, with the wool outside: this they wear just thrown over their shoulders, leaving their persons as often exposed as covered. Their skin is of a dirty coppery-red colour....."

"Their very attitudes were abject, and the expression of their countenances distrustful, surprised, and startled. After we had presented them with some scarlet cloth, which they immediately tied round their necks, they became good friends.

This was shown by the old man patting our breasts, and making a clucking kind of noise, as people do when feeding chickens. I walked with the old man, and this demonstration of friendship was repeated several times; it was concluded by three hard slaps, which were given me on the breast and back at the same time.

He then bared his bosom for me to return the compliment, which being done, he seemed highly pleased. The language of these people, according to our notions, scarcely deserves to be called articulate. Captain Cook has compared it to a man clearing his throat, but certainly no European ever cleared his throat with so many hoarse, guttural, and clicking sounds."

It seems that even for people as well travelled as the Beagle's crew, the Fuegians made a real impression; for being so different to any native peoples that they had encountered before:

"They are excellent mimics: as often as we coughed or yawned, or made any odd motion, they immediately imitated us. Some of our party began to squint and look awry; but one of the young Fuegians (whose whole face was painted black, excepting a white band across his eyes) succeeded in making far more hideous grimaces…

When a song was struck up by our party, I thought the Fuegians would have fallen down with astonishment. With equal surprise they viewed our dancing; but one of the young men, when asked, had no objection to a little waltzing. Little accustomed to Europeans as they appeared to be, yet they knew and dreaded our fire-arms; nothing would tempt them to take a gun in their hands. They begged for knives, calling them by the Spanish word cuchilla."

But although Darwin writes disparagingly of the people's 'savagery', their hardiness was to me truly astounding. To survive in a place as hostile to life as the tip of Patagonia, is nothing short of remarkable. Especially when taking into consideration their lack of clothing or housing:

"While going one day on shore near Wollaston Island, we pulled alongside a canoe with six Fuegians. These were the most abject and miserable creatures I anywhere beheld. On the east coast the natives, as we have seen, have guanaco cloaks, and on the west they possess seal-skins. Amongst these central tribes the men generally have an otter-skin, or some small scrap about as large as a pocket handkerchief, which is barely sufficient to cover their backs as low down as their loins. It is laced across the breast by strings, and according as the wind blows, it is shifted from side to side.

But these Fuegians in the canoe were quite naked, and even one full-grown woman was absolutely so. It was raining heavily, and the fresh water, together with the spray, trickled down her body. In another harbour not far distant, a woman, who was suckling a recently-born child, came one day alongside the vessel, and remained there out of mere curiosity, whilst the sleet fell and thawed on her naked bosom, and on the skin of her naked baby!"

"These poor wretches were stunted in their growth, their hideous faces bedaubed with white paint, their skins filthy and greasy, their hair entangled, their voices discordant, and their gestures violent. Viewing such men, one can hardly make one's self believe that they are fellow-creatures, and inhabitants of the same world. It is a common subject of conjecture what pleasure in life some of the lower animals can enjoy: how much more reasonably the same question may be asked with respect to these barbarians!

At night, five or six human beings, naked and scarcely protected from the wind and rain of this tempestuous climate, sleep on the wet ground coiled up like animals. Whenever it is low water, winter or summer, night or day, they must rise to pick shell-fish from the rocks; and the women either dive to collect sea-eggs, or sit patiently in their canoes, and with a baited hair-line without any hook, jerk out little fish. If a seal is killed, or the floating carcass of a putrid whale is discovered, it is a feast; and such miserable food is assisted by a few tasteless berries and fungi."

Whatever your thoughts on the nature of the explorers' regard for the native peoples, Darwin's account does give a useful insight into their habits and way of life in the early 19th century:

"The different tribes have no government or chief; yet each is surrounded by other hostile tribes, speaking different dialects, and separated from each other only by a deserted border or neutral territory: the cause of their warfare appears to be the means of subsistence. Their country is a broken mass of wild rocks, lofty hills, and useless forests: and these are viewed through mists and endless storms. The habitable land is reduced to the stones on the beach; in search of food they are compelled unceasingly to wander from spot to spot, and so steep is the coast, that they can only move about in their wretched canoes.

They cannot know the feeling of having a home, and still less that of domestic affection; for the husband is to the wife a brutal master to a laborious slave. Was a more horrid deed ever perpetrated, than that witnessed on the west coast by Byron, who saw a wretched mother pick up her bleeding dying infant-boy, whom her husband had mercilessly dashed on the stones for dropping a basket of sea-eggs.

How little can the higher powers of the mind be brought into play: what is there for imagination to picture, for reason to compare, for judgment to decide upon? to knock a limpet from

325

the rock does not require even cunning, that lowest power of the mind. Their skill in some respects may be compared to the instinct of animals; for it is not improved by experience: the canoe, their most ingenious work, poor as it is, has remained the same, as we know from Drake, for the last two hundred and fifty years."

Before leaving Navarino Island I wished to visit and pay my respects to one of these 'wretched savages', so I set off from Puerto Williams and marched eastward along the main road out of town.

I was going to look for a woman called Christina Calderon; a lady born in the 1920s who was rumoured to be the last pure-blooded descendant of the Yaghan people.

It wasn't long before I reached a small collection of homes in an area called Robalo. There was a patch of grass outside on which some children played. I approached one of them and explained the reason for my presence.

"Hola, Busco Senora Christina Calderon?" I said to a little boy.

"La Tia?" asked the boy, wanting to know if I was referring to his Aunt.

He led me up to the door to one of the nearby houses, and after a while a lady emerged. She had a weathered face and short greying-black hair, but did not seem particularly frail. In fact, she appeared to be in remarkably good health for someone who was at least in her late seventies. I certainly wouldn't think to describe her as an 'uncivilised savage!'

Suddenly nervous, I realised that I had very little to say to this lady, who now stared at me blankly. She was clearly wondering what it was that I wanted with her. I decided not to overplay my Englishness if asked where I was from, just in case my countrymen had anything to do with her race's demise.

I had anticipated that conversation would spontaneously ignite between us, but we both just stared at each other in a very awkward silence.

"So, errr, you're Yamana then?" I offered as a starter for ten.

"Yep" she replied monosyllabically.

"Ok, I want to talk to you because...." Oh god why did I want to talk to her? I desperately racked my brain for something uplifting to say.

"So, you're the last of your people then?" Was the best that I could come up with.

It is a good job that I wasn't looking for a date. Reminding someone of their race's extermination as soon as you meet them, doesn't really rank up there with the all-time great chat-up lines.

"Yes, well I have a few nieces who aren't here right now, but I am the last one who speaks the Yamana language". She said before continuing;

"But of course, I have no-one to speak it to" she said with a sad smile.

Somewhat overawed by the fact that I was conversing with a representative of a bygone era, and the last surviving member of an entire race of people, I then fell lost for words. Cristina seemed unwilling to fill the awkward void.

So, after a few more lines of small talk I decided that enough was enough. I said that it had been a pleasure to meet her and bid her farewell. Weaving my way through the children, I began to walk back towards Williams whilst being watched from the doorstep by Señora Calderon and three generations of her family.

I decided to spend my final night on Navarino in the wilderness away from humanity. I wanted to think back on all that had passed, and all that might await me in the future. So once again I shouldered my pack, stuffed as it was with plentiful food and drink, and walked off again in the direction of the 'Los Dientes' mountains.

I made my way once again past the saintly statue of the Virgin Mary, surrounded as she was by her abundantly flowered garden. I then continued up the same track that I had taken almost a week earlier when starting out on my expedition to Navarino's jagged teeth. This time though I followed the path for barely half an hour, before making a right turn into a heavily overgrown track.

I was looking for a secluded spot to spend the night. But try as I might, I could find nowhere in the dense undergrowth where there was room to pitch a tent. Eventually I decided to hide my belongings behind

329

some bushes at the side of the track, before going off to explore deeper into the forest away from the paths, and without the cumbersome burden of my bulky and heavy backpack. I hadn't gone far before the ground fell away sharply before me. I found myself stood on the lip of a small, but densely wooded cliff. I scrambled tentatively downwards, pausing regularly to climb over the many felled trees that obstructed my path. It was only a matter of minutes before I reached the bottom.

Confronting me now however was an even greater obstacle; a deep and powerfully fast-flowing river that ran perpendicular to my course. On the verge of turning back, I looked to the river's far bank and saw there a perfect camp site. Sheltered, isolated, and with a plentiful source of fresh water and firewood, it was exactly what I had been looking for. The problem now was how to get there.

The river was in fact the same one which came out from the hydroelectric dam in the hills above. The many dead tree trunks that had been swept along in its powerful current, were a testament to the raw power of its waters. Its shimmering currents lapped and swirled with a force born in the jagged peaks to the north. They surged forwards until they collided with one of the many log jams, where the water would gurgle and spray in protest, working their way through the barricades before continuing their short journey seaward.

After scouting up and down the river, searching in vain for an easy crossing point, I realised that the only way across was via the top of one of the log jams. I left my belongings on the riverbank and stepped onto the first log. My intention was to walk across the top of the logs as quickly as possible, maintaining my momentum, and therefore in theory my balance.

This plan was to fail exactly halfway across. I stepped onto a thin, badly supported log, that moved as soon as I put my weight upon it. Falling straight forwards, panic flared through me as I braced for the water's icy touch. Fortunately it never came, as I managed to land with both hands supporting me on a more stable part of the ramshackle log pile.

I continued the rest of the way crawling. I took a lot more care about where I was going, and on reaching the other side I was immediately able to see that it had been worth the effort. The area was a perfect camp-site. It was on a bend in the river so that three sides were surrounded by water, whilst the fourth was thick forest, making an ideal hideaway.

Re-crossing the river I climbed back up the cliff and fetched my belongings, before crossing a third time with some difficulty, then setting up camp. What was to follow was without doubt one of the most tranquil nights of my life. I was able to sit eating a large meal of pasta and sausages with a plentiful supply of biscuits and chocolate. I unashamedly stuffed myself.

With the sun shining brightly down, I listened to the river flowing beside me as I read the one book that I'd managed to bring; *'A Brief History of the Magellenes'*. It was amusing and at the same time sobering to read of the harrowing experiences of the first European explorers to visit these lands hundreds of years ago. I read of famines, disasters, massacres, sinkings, sackings, pirates and battles with Indians, that characterised the colonisation of this inhospitable land at the very end of the world. As the sun eventually began to sink below the horizon, I started a fire that became so fierce that I was able to pull logs from the river that had been submerged for years in water, and before long have them burning like the rest.

When night finally fell, I saw that the sky was full of the brightest clearest stars the like of which I had never seen. The constellations shone with a radiant brightness that made them seemingly come alive. I could clearly make out other galaxies, hanging an incomprehensible distance away though the vastness of space. Eventually I crawled into my sleeping bag, sealed the tent door and spent the following twenty minutes squashing the various mosquitoes that always seemed to somehow find their way inside.

Whilst drifting off to sleep, I realised that I had probably never been so at peace. There I was, on an island so far south that even most Chileans hadn't heard of it. I was sleeping in a place where nobody knew where I was, and a person would have trouble getting to me even if they did. In a way I was in a portal of the mind between two journeys.

I had decided that my time in Chile must soon come to an end. I continued to love every moment that I had spent in that extreme country, and the company of its people who were so unthinkingly generous with their love and friendship. But I could feel the need to find a

333

role for myself in life, and English teaching didn't seem to be it.

My time with the Chilean Army had been one of the most enjoyable and inspiring weeks of my life. I began to think that maybe as I had done it for a week, I could do it for a career? The news was full of people procrastinating about how best to solve the problems in the world, but it seemed to me that the military were one of the few groups prepared to try to do something practical about them. So, painful as the decision was, I decided to return home and try to join the Army while I was still relatively young and unburdened.

Firstly though I had unfinished business in Chile. I had seen raging seas, towering mountains, glistening glaciers, and native peoples steeped in tradition. But no journey through Chile would be complete without a trip to the far North. Up there were lands of scorching sands, boiling geysers and mirage-spattered salt plains. So I decided that on my way home I would stop off at the Atacama: the driest desert in the world.

After a big breakfast the following morning, I dismantled the camp-site and plodded the five miles or so to the airport. The same small aircraft that I'd come in on carried me back towards Punta Arenas. On this flight I suffered none of the queasiness that I'd experienced on the way in, but was more than a little perturbed by a series of loud bangs coming from the aircraft's fuselage.

It sounded like the plane was coming apart at the seams. But the pilot explained by shouting through the open cockpit doorway, that it was chunks of ice impacting against the aircraft's thin aluminium skin. I was very sad to leave Navarino Island, and sadder still that this trip was to take me onto the final leg of my journey, and then eventually away from Chile itself.

A Caustic Emptiness

I didn't want to leave Chile and end my odyssey before seeing the country's arid North. So I decided to visit the desert region that borders Peru and Bolivia; a part of the country that was thousands of kilometres from the Araucania that I had come to know as home.

Time, as ever, was tight. I only had a few days to see the sights of the North before my flight to the UK would depart from Santiago, and in that time there was much to achieve. In the part of Chile that surrounds the Tropic of Capricorn, there exists salt plains resplendent with hordes of pink flamingos, sand dunes as high as mountains, ancient artefacts from desert tribes, volcanoes, mountains and geysers which erupt from the parched ground with broiling intensity.

After spending half a day in the coastal city of Antofagasta, admiring rock formations and monuments to a colonial past, I boarded a coach that would take me right through the heart of the desert, to a place called San Pedro de Atacama. San Pedro was once an unknown desert village, but it was rapidly becoming one of the North's tourist hotspots. It was a base for expeditions and trips into the wider desert and a destination in itself, with bars, shops, a renowned archaeological museum and the second oldest church in Chile. I wasn't really going there for any of those things though. The main purpose of my visit was to catch an apparently exquisite sunset, that occurs in the remote tranquillity of a place named; The Valley of the Moon.

My coach began to slow down before turning off the highway onto a wide, but rough and un-surfaced, desert track. Eventually, small single-story dwellings of a basic brick and mud construction hove into view, breaking-up the desert's emptiness. We seemed to be passing through a small settlement. It resembled the sort of place that one would expect to find in the Middle East, or perhaps North Africa. It had a simple attractiveness

337

that was quite different to the overwhelming beauty of the national parks throughout Chile's south.

There were several stalls by the side of the road and one of the huts had a Tur-Bus sign nailed above its doorway; Tur Bus being one of Chile's most reputable national coach companies. It had been a long journey to get there, but I began to think that I might have finally arrived at my destination.

My suspicions were confirmed by the increasing presence of tourists and backpackers on the barren streets. It was hard to believe that that two days prior I had been building a snowman in the mountains of Chile's south on Christmas Eve. Now here I was spending Boxing Day in the scorching heat of the world's driest desert.

San Pedro was sandwiched between the sprawling mining town of Calama, and the Andes mountain range. It is surrounded on all sides by the Atacama Desert, for some areas of which there are no records of any rain having fallen, ever. Despite the remoteness of the town, it was very popular with tourists and formed a part of the itinerary of many a traveller. It was often visited by tourists before they headed onward and upwards into the great Bolivian salt planes.

As I was only to be there for one night and evening was fast approaching, I had to get a move on if I was to make it to the Valley of the Moon before sunset. The priority was to find some accommodation. This was something that proved easy, as I was recruited to a hostel practically the second that I stepped off the coach.

This probably wasn't the best technique to find the optimum place to stay. But as long as the place was cheap, had a bed, a loo and a shower, I was not too bothered about the specifics or other home comforts. The woman who was to take me to the hostel suddenly started pointing at a guy a few metres behind me. Another backpacker; his features suggested to me that he was South American, from Peru or Bolivia I deduced, so of course, he turned out to be Japanese.

"Es tu amigo?" she asked, but I explained that no, I had never met him before. She then approached him and asked the pair of us if we would like to share a room as it would be cheaper. I had no problem with this and neither did he, so she proceeded to lead us through

the dusty back streets until we arrived at the large wooden gates of her hostel.

It consisted of a basic series of rooms surrounding a central courtyard, which contained little but a few parched-looking palm trees. Between the two trees was strung a large hammock, in which relaxed an attractive blond tourist who barely raised her head from her book as we passed on by. Despite the sparseness, the place was clean, had a laid-back atmosphere about it, and at £3.50 a night I had no reason to complain.

My new Japanese amigo was from Osaka, but I had little time to get to know him more. It seemed that the only thing that he had planned for the remainder of the day, was the resting of his eyelids.

That was a luxury which I couldn't afford, if I was to see the Valley of The Moon that night and still get to Chucuicamata[1] the following day. Making my way to the town's main street, I strove to find a tour company able to take me out into the desert. They certainly

---

[1] The world's largest open cut mine.

appeared to be in no short supply. It was however at that point that my problems started. After visiting every agency in town, it soon became apparent that none of them would be running any more tours that day.

I decided to ask someone in one of the more adventurous looking agencies, if there was any possible way that I could get to the Moon Valley in time for sundown that same night.

"Well you could cycle there…" was the agent's guarded reply.

I sceptically asked how far away it was; it seemed strange to me that so few people cycled if it was within an easily achievable distance.

"About eleven kilometres" was his curt response.

By then it was nearly a quarter past six in the evening, and the sun was due to set at a quarter past eight. So I would have about an hour and a half to do eleven kilometres through the desert, which, although far from easy, did indeed sound feasible.

341

I decided to risk it and the man from the agency kindly agreed to escort me to his recommended bike shop. As he led me along the narrow, dusty main street he asked where I was from:

"Soy Ingles" I replied. I returned the question, expecting the answer to be a country in northern Europe due to his fair skin and light, almost blond hair.

"Chileano" he answered, with a look on his face that said I had just asked the world's stupidest question.

On arrival at the bike rental shop, I enquired as to the absolute latest possible time I could return the bike that evening, and ten o'clock was the reply. I was unsuccessful in my attempts to negotiate a later return, and the realisation dawned that there would be very little room for error on this trip.

I made sure to give the bike a thorough testing. The last thing that I wanted was a repeat of an experience that I'd had previously on a visit to the southern coastal town of Ancud. On which occasion I'd found myself hurtling downhill out of control on a worn-out bicycle, with no functioning brakes. A bicycle that seemed to have been made for a person roughly the size of a Hobbit.

This time though, the bike proved to be excellent; good gears, solid brakes and seemingly sturdy enough to withstand the journey ahead. My watch told me that it was six thirty by the time I finally managed to set off, and with the tight time constraints that I was under I knew that this was going to be a real rushed job. I had hoped to spend a few hours out in the desert, soaking in the atmosphere. But I now realised that I'd be lucky just to see the sunset, and get back in time to make it out of San Pedro and on to mining town of Calama the next day.

After leaving the deeply rutted dirt track of the high street and heading north out of town, I joined the main highway back to Calama which I would be following for much of the coming hour. The highway was a good modern one, on which I expected to make good progress. However, there was one problem. It seemed to pass over the top what looked to me like a small mountain. It was in fact just a very large hill, but a hill nevertheless that was a darn sight larger than the one Jack and Jill had fallen down.

343

The road wound its way up the edge of the cliff and seemed to get ever steeper. It was at least a twenty percent incline and I quickly grew tired, stopping every two hundred metres for a rest and a drink. Water was not something that I had skimped on, having four litres with me altogether. This may seem like overkill for a journey of only a few hours, and indeed it probably was. But the Atacama Desert is the driest in the entire world, some parts of it have never seen rainfall. So water was not something that it would have paid to cut corners on.

After an hour of painfully tiring pedalling, I made it to the top of the hill and found that the view at the summit was certainly worth the effort. From where I then stood the Andes, which must have been at least eighty kilometres away, were easily visible. In their midst was the distant beautiful cone of the Licancabur volcano. But there wasn't a lot of time to admire the scenery, because unlikely as it was that I'd make it to the moon valley, I still had to try.

As my eyes fell on the road ahead my spirit was soon lifted. A great desolate valley now lay in front of me, but the road from this point onwards appeared to be all downhill. It stretched out ahead as straight as an arrow, and went on seemingly forever. It continued as far as I could see, before disappearing into the haze on the far horizon. I only needed to follow it for a few miles before turning off into the national park. So I should easily have been able to make it in time, with barely a need to even pedal.

As I pushed off into the vast valley, I was entering an area eloquently described by Brian Keenan in his book Between Extremes:

"The place was grim beyond belief. As I walked around it trying to get a sense of its caustic emptiness words fell from me in despair. This environment was ugly and hostile, a lamentable landmass that would give no respite to my loathing of it. For the life of me, I couldn't understand why we, or anyone else would wish to see it. This was a vista of total corruption."

And this from somebody who spent five years of his life in a Lebanese prison cell, making him a man of experience in places *'grim beyond belief'.*

Looking back on it I do find this description slightly harsh, perhaps Brian had been suffering from an unusual bout of depression that day. However, I could appreciate where his sentiments were coming from, especially where the *'caustic emptiness'* was concerned. It was a place of utter lifelessness. Not a cactus or piece of moss in sight, just dust, sand, gravel and rocks, which seemed to stretch out in all directions as far as the eye could see.

I coasted down the lonely desert road, that appeared to continue straight as an arrow all the way to the far horizon. But the journey down into the valley proved considerably harder than I had expected. This was due to the powerful uphill wind that rose up to confront me from the distant valley floor. I now had a big problem, as I had been hoping for a very fast downhill run to make for the time lost earlier. As the wind became increasingly stronger my temperament grew angrier. The realisation began to dawn on me that I possibly was to have my goal snatched away from me at the last hurdle.

By now the strength of the wind had become exasperating; it was so powerful that I could barely even keep my eyes on the road ahead. I decided out of curiosity to take my feet off the bicycle's pedals, and surely enough I rolled scarcely a few metres onward before the bike came coasting to a halt, despite the road going steeply downhill.

It was now twenty minutes to sundown. I realised that with the almighty wind I didn't stand a cat in hell's chance of making it to the Valle de la Luna in time for the renowned sunset. I was so frustrated at being foiled by a force as seemingly innocuous as the wind, that I began to scream every obscenity that I knew, and a few I invented especially for the occasion, up at the heavens and out into the great beyond. But I received no reply to my foul-tempered tirade from either celestial or terrestrial being. It is said that, *'in space, no one can hear you scream'.* Well it also seems that in the Atacama Desert; no one can hear you swear!

It must then have been ten minutes before sunset. The sun was very low in the sky, it was about as low as the morale in my heart. I had failed in my goal. The desert, so devoid of any form of life, was the ultimate depressant.

Then a sudden thought occurred to me. The sunset was supposed to be beautiful from the valley of the

347

moon, and I was only a few kilometres away from there. Surely the sunset would be spectacular from this location also? I then saw that off to my left there was a tall brown spire of rock, standing alone in the wilderness like a monument to a cause long forgotten. The Sun's waning disc had already sunk low enough to kiss the tip of its spindly summit.

The best course of action open to me suddenly seemed obvious. I would hide the bike from the road behind a sand dune, then hike to the rocky spire that looked to be barely a hundred and fifty metres away, climb it, then watch the sunset from the very top of it. What could possibly go wrong?

With the sun continuing to rapidly sink, I carried the bike to a spot behind a large pile of loose, slatey rock, and hid it. I tried to ensure that it was completely invisible from the road, but would still be easy enough for me to spot upon my eventual return.

After ditching the bike, I began to jog across the broken shale. There were scant minutes left until sundown, and after all of the travelling and effort that I had been through, I could not permit myself to miss it. Seemingly Mother Nature had other plans though; I had got barely any distance at all before all of a sudden the ground opened up before me. The hidden gorge which lay across my path was not a major obstacle, it was twenty metres across and the sides were barely three metres tall, but it was going to cost me precious time that I did not have. Having already failed in my main personal objective, I didn't want an unexpected gorge to stop me from achieving my new one.

Scrambling down the first part of the slope and jumping the rest, I landed heavily on my booted feet due to the extra weight of the pack on my back. Next was a dash across the valley floor and a fairly easy climb up the opposing wall. I then renewed my run towards the rocky spire. Despite my haste, I remained mindful to be very careful where I placed my feet. In the loose shale one could easily have twisted or broken an ankle, which would have left me stranded in the desert with no hope of medical aid

The sun had already set from where I was standing, but from the top of the spire it must surely still have been visible. I reckoned that by the skin of my teeth I was just going to make it. Then unbelievably another gorge, a carbon copy of the first, opened up before me.

I jumped straight off the edge without hesitation and landed with a roll in the soft sand and gravel at the bottom. Running as fast as I could across the valley floor, literally racing the sun, I scrambled up the opposite wall. A few of metres further on and I was at what seemed to be the base of the spire.

Every second now crucial, I ditched my backpack due to its extra weight. Considering that the pack contained all of my water, a compass, torch, food and many other survival aids, this could have been incredibly unwise. But the spire seemed to be literally right next to me and only about six metres tall. Surely nothing could possibly go wrong now?

At the base of the column I saw that there was a deep groove in the side of the cliff which prevented me from going further. I would have to climb the tower of rock via an awkward spiral route, much like a circus slide in reverse. A thought began to tease itself into my mind that being without my pack for any length of time in the desert really was a stupid thing to do. But I pushed this notion away as I wanted nothing to stop me from reaching my goal.

It was now twenty past eight; five minutes later than the time that I had been told the sun was due to set. I kept climbing, sure that I was only seconds away from the summit. Never had six metres seemed to take such a long time to scale. Finally at the top, I sat down and gazed out across a landscape of bleak desolation, given life only by the last rays of a fading sun. I continued to watch whilst dangling my booted legs out into the vast open space below.

During the few minutes that it took for the sun to finish its journey earthward, it changed from a warm yellow glow, to sharp orange rays that lanced outwards across the sky. They stabbed outwards from the far horizon in a final protest, before being swallowed up by the earth like a sinner falling to perdition.

All that remained afterwards was a soft pink glow, which mingled gently with the bright moonlight and intense twinkling of the stars.

After sitting alone in total silence for some time, I became mindful of what would happen if I was in the desert with no pack when the sun went down. I stayed for as long as possible, then started to climb down the

351

spire before turning my back on one of the most tranquil places that I had ever encountered.

Now the race was truly on. I had to find my pack at all costs and there was only one, maybe two minutes of the sun's afterglow left. There was no option but to run back that way that I had come as fast I could. The loose shale underfoot proved itself very treacherous, but my concerns over safety now paled in comparison to the fear of being stuck in the middle of the desert at night with no water.

It was virtually dark by the time that I spotted a small lump in the middle distance. It was not exactly where I had expected it to be, but was sufficiently alien-looking against its backdrop to convince me that it was indeed my pack. Feeling relieved and sure that the more serious of my problems were over, I threw the bag over my shoulder and began to trek back in the direction of the highway.

All I then needed to do was to find my bike and make my way home; a task that seemed at the time as though it would be as simple as shooting fish in a barrel. After I had crossed the cursed hidden valleys that had delayed me so much on the way out, the main road seemed so close that I felt I could almost reach out and touch it. Time was now so short that I was fairly doubtful that I'd make it back to San Pedro for the ten o'clock deadline, but I intended to give it my best shot.

Then, of course, my cursed bike was nowhere to be found.

I felt certain that I was in the correct part of the desert and sure that the bike couldn't be further than a hundred metres away in any particular direction. But despite all my searching it still failed to materialise. I had on my person a rugged and trusty metal torch, but in the blackness the weak beam that shone from its tiny filament bulb, was only able to penetrate the night out to a few metres.

Up and down the desert I walked, stress levels getting higher and higher as time wore on. I was confident that I was not in any serious danger, at maximum it was a three hour walk to San Pedro, and the main road was fairly easy to locate due to the lights of the occasional passing truck.

However, after thirty minutes of constantly wandering up and down the same stretch of featureless desert, I began to run very low on both energy and morale. It felt as though the night had somehow swallowed the bike up whole.

Soon the ridiculous possibility entered my mind that the bike could have been stolen. But even accepting the tiny possibility that someone else would be in the same part of the desert as me at that time, it would surely have taken a very malicious kind of a person to steal somebody's only form of transport in the middle of a hostile desert. I refused to accept that anyone could or would have stolen the bike, and resigned myself to continuing my fruitless and depressing search.

After traipsing back and forth whilst straining my vision for signs of anything out of place in the environment, I looked at my watch and noticed that I'd been searching that small patch of nothingness for an hour. My torch was fading, as was my will to carry on, so it was time to decide what to do. There seemed to be three options open to me; I could go back to the town and admit that I'd lost the bike. But as well as looking totally stupid, I'd probably end up paying the 'gringo' price for a replacement. This would be far in excess of anything that I, as an English teacher living on little more than a subsistence wage, would be able to afford.

Perhaps I should just grab my bag and jump on the next bus out of town. But apart from the negative moral implications of this course of action, it would have meant that I wouldn't ever be able to return to San Pedro. Also the bike rental place had taken down my passport number, so I could be faced with some awkward questions when I eventually did try to leave the country.

The third option seemed to be the least dire; a three hour walk back to town, four hours sleep, followed by another walk out into the desert at first light to continue my search. This course of action was one that was far from perfect though; it would drive me to exhaustion, and there would still be no guarantee that I'd find the bike at the end of it all. But it felt like my only real option, so I turned around and began the long trek back to the village.

It was only at this point that I realised how light it had become. Off to the East the full moon had risen high into the sky. It was now shining down brightly, illuminating the landscape for miles around like a miniature monochrome sun. Even under those miserable circumstances it was breath-taking, a pity that it was not quite bright enough to really aid me in my fruitless search.

I was still thinking about the beautiful and surreal nature of a moon that thinks it is a sun, when something suddenly made me freeze in my tracks. The beam of my torch had revealed a small groove cut into the sand in front of me.

I'm surprised that I even noticed it, but something about the shape of that indentation in a small ridge of sand seemed out of place; as if it were not naturally formed but instead was man-made.

After following the groove for a few metres, I came across a boot-print in the sand. Studying the tread pattern revealed that it was one of mine. Despite this discovery I tried not to get my hopes up. My boot-prints were all over that part of the desert, as I must have walked up and down it a thousand times on that long and lonely night.

Then the waning beam of my almost dead torch reflected off something small in the middle distance. Either I had seen one of the mirages so common in children's' cartoons, or perhaps the efforts of the previous hours were sending me slightly insane.

Running towards the source of illumination, my heart almost jumped out of my mouth as revealed to me in all its glory was indeed the lost bicycle's rear reflector! I felt utterly elated, a massive burden suddenly lifted from my tired and aching shoulders. I felt an urge to celebrate. The only way that I could think of to do so was to take a blurry and dark photo of the two-wheeled friend with whom I had almost parted company for good.

After wheeling the bike across broken ground back to the desert road, I began to cycle back up the long slope to the top of the hill which had caused me so much trouble on the way out. Cliffs soon rose up on either side, blocking out most of the moonlight. It was so dark that the only way to keep in a straight line was by following the dashed white lines in the middle of the road.

Ten minutes later and I had already reached the summit of the hill, a far shorter time than it had taken me to cycle down it on the way out. I put this partly down to the fact that the darkness had hidden from me how far I had left to go, so I just peddled and peddled without stopping for frequent breaks. Now though was

357

time for the fun part. With the steep downward gradient on the other side, and the wind at my back, I was able to fly down the hill at a phenomenal speed. I hurtled along faster than I'd ever been on a bicycle before. It took all of my concentration just to hold on tightly to the handlebars, whilst trying to keep the bike pointed in a straight line.

At the right-hand side of the road was a low metal barrier, of the sort that are common on British motorways. On the other side of this was a sheer drop of what looked to me to be about half a kilometre downwards. It was a huge expanse of still air, broken only by the jagged mountain peaks in the far distance, and the dust strewn desert floor an almost imperceptible distance below.

However this was not a major worry. I could take the corners easily enough as I had both lanes of the road all to myself. Besides, I didn't really want to try the brakes, because at the speed I was going I wasn't exactly sure what would happen.

It was at this point that I saw the bright white lights of the oncoming pickup truck.

Now normally this wouldn't have been too much of a problem. But it soon became evident that I would be passing the truck on a tight corner, one that was situated on the cliff edge, which greatly reduced my margin of error. Still, as long as I remained in control and didn't panic, I felt confident in my ability to make the turn.

The truck closed the distance rapidly and left little time for thought before being upon me. It was less than a second away before my nerves finally failed me. Feeling that I must lose some speed or crash over the edge of the cliff, I squeezed the rear brake lever as gently as I felt able, but it was still not gently enough.

The rear wheel locked and wrenched itself viscously sideways, as if it had been yanked by some malicious invisible hand. This was an *'oh shit moment'*; a tiny fraction of a second when your brain is in shock and not consciously in control of your body. The way that you react in these instances is controlled by something deep within the subconscious.

I completely let go of the brakes; a reaction that was to save my life as it caused the rear wheel to be pulled back into line at the same moment that I passed by the truck. All of this must have happened in less than half a second, but it took considerably longer than that for my breath to return to normal and for my heart to stop racing.

The bike straightening itself caused one of the metal pedals to bite into my calf. It was a small price to pay, but the marks from the pedal's pointed teeth were still present several months later. Rounding the corner, I continued down the hill, albeit at a slightly slower pace than before. The momentum that I built up kept me going all the way to the outskirts of San Pedro. My watch displayed ten o'clock. Unbelievably it seemed that I would be going to make it just in the nick of time.

I tore down the main street as people were starting to go out for the night. They were nearly all foreigners; no self-respecting Chilean would even think about leaving the house to party until gone midnight. I slowed down for none of them, weaving through a human slalom of tourists and occasional locals, a trail of dust left in my wake. Breathing a massive sigh of relief, I arrived back at the rental shop and returned the bicycle, looking down at my watch I saw that it read five past ten.

Returning the bike signified a welcome end to the day's adventuring. The sensible thing to do then would have been to get an early night, so that I would rise first thing the following morning to make full use of the day.

However, drinking nothing but water all day, losing the bike, and almost becoming the first gringo to fly across the Atacama on a bicycle, and in the process looking like a taller, whiter and infinitely more terrified version of ET, had made me thirsty.

Despite the poor and slightly third-world appearance of San Pedro, the tourist trade had obviously benefited the town immensely. One of those benefits was a plentiful supply of bars catering to every taste, whether warm and cosy, or lively and full of character. There was something there to suit everyone.

Walking up and down the main street revealed quite a variety of watering holes. I opted for one that appeared to be very popular. It had fairly loud Latino music blaring out, and a large open fire in the centre. A quick look around at the clientele and it seemed that most people were sat chatting in quite close-knit groups, so I took a seat by myself at the bar.

"Una cerveza por favor!" were the happiest words that I had said all day.

361

The only beer that they served was Crystal, and in cans at that. Now I'd like to mention that there are many Chilean beers that I came to adore. Escudo; a flavoursome lager named with the Spanish word for shield, was one, and of course there was Kunstmann; the fine beer that I had become closely acquainted with when I visited its hometown of Valdivia. However, I'm afraid that can't say really the same for Crystal. Still, at that point a beer was a beer, and I rapidly sank two of them before getting bored and moving on to glasses of the devilish brew that is Piscola; Pisco mixed with Coca Cola.

The time had come to make an important decision. Was I to leave first thing in the morning for Chuquicamata? Or, did I give up on the mine and take one of the guided tours to the Moon Valley proper? Thinking that I would rather witness the natural phenomenon than the man made one, I decided to leave Chuquicamata for another time. Impressive though it was sure to be, it was still basically just a giant man made whole in the ground. Besides, if I were to leave San Pedro directly after the trials and tribulations of the day that I'd just experienced, I would always feel that I had left some business unfinished.

Chatting for a while to the guy next to me at the bar, revealed that he worked as a senior manager for the ferry company that runs tours from the great island of Chiloe, down to Patagonia and Tierra del Fuego. It was a strange feeling to be thinking of the iceberg infested fjords and freezing mountains of that region at that time, surrounded as I was by dry sand and sun-baked rock in all directions.

Unfortunately, he disappeared before I could get him drunk enough to offer me any free tickets. So I returned my attentions to watching the amusing attempts of the local barman to impress his clientele, with some energetic cocktail mixing antics.

By this time, it was getting very late and I had lost count of how many piscolas had passed my lips. *'Just one more and then time to hit the road'* I decided. It was then that one of the locals took a seat next to me at the bar. He was similar in appearance to the beach Mapuche that I encountered down in Puerto Saavedra, and just as keen to communicate.

363

However, this time the atmosphere was different, somehow more menacing, and the Piscolas had taken full effect leaving me vulnerable. Due to my inebriated and tired state, and the way that the chap's 'mates' seemed to be suddenly clustered all around me, coupled to the fact that I was carrying my passport, wallet and an expensive mobile phone, I began to feel slightly threatened. This wasn't really helped when one of them turned to me and leant close until his face was inches from mine. Practically breathing down my neck, he started saying *"marihuana, marihuana"* with a wild stare in his eyes.

Did they think I had weed to sell them? The confusion was unnerving. I tried to reply with something fairly non-committal, but judging by their reactions I obviously wasn't non-committal enough. They pointed to each other and then to me, *"dos cervesas"*, was their demand. At 50p a can, a pound seemed to be a small price to pay to get me out of the awkward and tense situation that I now somehow found myself in.

The beer soon arrived and seemed to be appreciated by my dodgy new 'amigos'. So much so that one of them pulled my hand beneath the bar and emptied about two joints worth of the intoxicating weed into it.

"Ah muchas gracias, marihuana muy bein!" I declared probably far too loudly.

Realising that it was now time to leave, I paid for the drinks and staggered home, more drunk than I had felt for a long time. Somehow I made it back to the hostel, stumbled into bed, and passed out into a blessed unconsciousness.

On waking the next morning I was amazed to discover that I was in fact still alive. Even if the pounding in my head, sick feeling in my stomach and very high temperature throughout my body were doing their best to convince me otherwise.

I rolled out of bed and was relieved to find that I still had most of my possessions. So I headed out in search of a shower. I was to be disappointed as there seemed to be no running water in the hostel that morning. I threw on some clothes and returned to the main street to find some food. All of the time I was fighting back a nagging urge to vomit all over the road, in front of the various groups of sightseers who were out for a morning stroll.

Heading into the first café that I found, I purchased and rapidly drank a litre of orange juice under the bemused gaze of the café owner. Then I left in search of a breakfast that I would hopefully be able to keep down. Ducking inside one of the small artisanship markets, I found it cluttered with the usual assortment of locally made jewellery, clothes, and hand crafted ornaments, along with the more standard tourist offerings such as post cards and t-shirts.

In the middle of it all I found what I was really looking for; an ice-cream shop with a wide array of flavours and portion sizes. As my tortured stomach was now telling me that it was kill or cure time, I ordered the largest portion of the freshest tasting fruity ice cream available, savouring the smooth flavour as it slowly worked its hangover-dissolving magic.

Shopping around, I was able to find a company that would take me over to the Valle de la Luna, and I made sure to check that I'd arrive back in time to catch the bus to Calama. This was vital if I was to meet the plane that will take me to Santiago, and from there homeward.

After boarding a small minibus, I was told that the tour group was due to make two stops before reaching

Moon Valley. On our arrival at the first we pulled to the side of the road. I was shocked to discover that it was the same place where I had almost sailed over the edge of the cliff the night before. We stood admiring the impressive vista for ten minutes. This was all accompanied by a spirited commentary from the Chilean guide.

Getting back on the bus we continued for a while before pulling up to a gap in the cliff wall, whereupon we dismounted and walked down into what opened up to be an ancient valley. Its high walls showed countless layers of different types of rock deposits, evidence of a span of time beyond human comprehension.

Before entering, I noted that the valley entrance was very close to the area in which I had been stranded the previous night. This piece of information would not be particularly interesting, had the tour guide not informed me that the name of the place was 'The Valley of Death!'

The Valley of Death walk turned out to be actually a rather pleasant one. In between gazing up at the desiccated valley walls and piles of flaky wind-sculpted rock, I chatted idly to an American student whom I'd met on the minibus. It turned out that she was quite young, around nineteen, and was undertaking a placement year in the Argentinean capital of Buenos Aires. Soon we were back on the bus again and off to our final destination. Paying a small fee to enter the park, we first pulled up at a unique rock formation known as the Tres Marias (Three Marys).

Remarkably the wind had worn the rock down over time to depict, with spooky accuracy, three representations of the Virgin Mary in various poses. I wondered if perhaps the shaping of this sculpture was at any point aided by human hands, as it almost seemed a little too real to be a natural phenomenon. Although to the average staunchly Catholic Chilean mind, it was undoubtedly a miraculous work of the good lord.

The leftmost Mary appeared as if she was sheltering beneath a large rock, clutching a baby, whilst the one on the right kneeled with hands clasped to the front as if deep in prayer. In between them both stood tall the third depiction, once again seeming to have an infant in her arms, bundled up in a shroud of blankets. Then again, perhaps I merely possess an overly fertile imagination.

Around this time I started to grow increasingly anxious. The departure time was rapidly approaching for my coach out of San Pedro and on to the sprawling mining town of Calama. It was a coach that it was absolutely vital for me to catch, as my flight to Santiago, and subsequently England, was due to leave the following lunchtime from Antofagasta. Missing that coach could mean missing the plane, leaving me stuck in Chile with no foreseeable way home.

Despite receiving assurances from the tour company before heading out on this trip that we would get back in time, I got my student friend to ask the guide what time we were expected to return. To my immense consternation the reply was about half an hour later than the departure time for my coach!

After I expressed my displeasure at the situation, the guide offered to take me immediately back to San Pedro so that I'd catch the coach but miss the sunset again. After thinking it over I decided to continue with the tour, my guidebook to Chile mentioned one last bus from Calama that should get me to the Antofagasta in time, later than I would want, but still enabling me to catch the flight.

Heading off with my American companion, we began to climb up the side of a vast sand dune. It was so long and tall, that the people making their way along its apex appeared as mere specks far off in the distance. After ten minutes of climbing, it was our turn to walk in single file atop the dune's crest, following a column of tourists walking towards the rocky ridge ahead.

To the left and to the right the sands of the great dune fell sharply away down sheer slopes, that continued all the way down to the plateau on which our, now minute, minibuses awaited. The dune terminated in a rocky wall that proved fairly easy to climb, and it was at the top that we got our first glimpse of the impressive vista which awaited us.

Stretching out for what seemed like a hundred miles was a rocky landscape. It appeared as if it had been lifted from the very surface of the moon and deposited in this place millennia ago, remaining unchanged ever since. Finding a place to sit, I was surprised to see my Japanese roommate from the hostel pass by. On seeing me he gave me an enthusiastic greeting and continued onwards in search of his own spot.

Over a period of about ten minutes, the distant fiery ball of the sun sank unerringly on its daily voyage below the far horizon, bathing the valley before me in a surreal orange glow. The ranks of tourists to my left and right duly snapped away with an assortment of cameras. But despite the sights before me, my heart wasn't really in it. Looking back on it I had much preferred the solitude and personal discovery of the preceding night, despite the misfortunes that had accompanied it. As the last of the light faded from the night sky, we turned and retraced our steps down the great dune, back to the minibuses below for the journey back to town.

I had indeed missed the coach that would have got me out of San Pedro, and subsequently down to Antofagasta on time to catch my flight the next morning. However, I managed to jump on one that would take me half-way. So I duly arrived in the mining town of Calama late the same night. Calama is a sprawling desert town that is home to approximately one hundred and thirty thousand people. The majority of whom are the workers and associated relatives of the nearby Chucuicamata copper mine; the largest open pit mine in the world.

The Chucuicamata mine is one of Chile's most important economic assets. In the year 2000 it was

371

responsible for five percent of the entire world's copper output. It is around nine hundred meters deep, has a surface area of around eight million square meters, and produces around six hundred and fifty thousand metric tons of copper per year. The mine is so large that in 2003 it swallowed the adjacent town of the same name. The residents were forced to move to Calama.

But it is not just those who get excited about big numbers who would find interest in the place. It has historical significance as an area where the ancient Aymara native peoples used the surface copper deposits to form basic weapons and tools. More recently it was visited by Ernesto "Che" Guevara on his motorcycle tour of South America. During his visit he witnessed terrible exploitation of the people by governmental and American corporations. This influenced the forming of his Marxist ideals, and inspired him to take up his lifelong revolutionary cause.

The city's motto is 'Calama; land of sun and copper'. Hardly the most inspirational motto of all time, but then Calama is not exactly an inspiring city. I said once that there is not a single part of Chile that I was not fond of; Calama however is a notable exception. Despite its location in an area of technological, historical and political significance, I found it to be an ugly, boring, dirty desert town with scant few attractions. An Israeli traveller once exclaimed to me upon hearing that I was spending most of my time in Temuco; *"but that place is a shithole!"* Well for me it was Calama that held the dubious honour of that description.

Generally, in Chile's cities there are large numbers of stray dogs that wander the streets throughout day and night, but Calama seemed to possess them in vast quantities. In fact, as soon as I disembarked from the coach into the city's soulless bus depot, I encountered several such specimens winding their way through the crowd in the futile hope of being thrown a little food. I paid them scant attention at that stage and headed straight for the depot reception area. I prayed that I would find a way to get to Antofagasta that very same night.

The news however was not good, there were to be no more coaches that night and, contrary to what it said in my guidebook, the next departure was not to be until nine o'clock the next morning. This would be far too late for me to stand a chance of making my flight in time, and therefore departing the country. Was it possible that I would be stuck in the hole that was Calama forever?

With that terrible thought I trudged out into the city in search of a different depot. Coaches in Chile usually depart from the major cities several times throughout the night, so I remained optimistic despite the apparent setback. There were however several potential pitfalls in my path. Calama was the only Chilean city in my guidebook for which I had no map, it had little tourist infrastructure and a reputation for a high crime rate. It was said to be dangerous at night; which it then was, and especially for gringos; which I am.

I tried to remain undaunted. Despite it being past midnight, I roamed the city streets. My shoulders strained under the weight of my two heavy backpacks, whilst I followed the occasional coach in search of any way to Antofagasta. I continued like this for about two hours. During this time I passed two bus stations; both totally shut. I found the town centre which was also virtually deserted, with the exception of a few dejected tramps, and walked a not inconsiderable number of miles around the silently threatening streets.

Eventually I found myself back where I started at the bus depot. I felt defeated and fatigued with aching feet, legs, back, shoulders and head. By then (around two in the morning) the place was completely locked. So I went around to the front, sat down upon a low wall and began to ponder my future course of action. I was soon joined by a trio of scruffy street-dogs (known locally as perros vaga bundos; tramp dogs), the very same ones that I had seen in the depot upon my arrival.

Clearly they wanted food, perhaps they could smell the crumbling biscuits inside my pack. All three of them stank, and like most stray dogs, they were absolutely filthy. God knows what diseases and bugs they carried. Despite their friendly inquisitiveness, I made sure to keep them at arm's length. I resolved not to feed them, in fear that I might never shake them off.

The biggest of the three was around two feet long and had a large grey coat of mangy fur which was heavily matted with dirt and grease. He had earlier seemed well known to the bus depot staff. I guess that he was something of a permanent fixture there, helped no doubt by his friendly disposition. Presumably he was

375

once a treasured family pet with cute fluffy hair, but now his only way to survive was to scrounge the streets for scraps, like the many thousands of other stray dogs in Chile.

His companions consisted of a tiny, brown 'handbag' type dog, who must only have survived on the streets thus far thanks to the support of the other hounds in the pack, and a young German Shepherd. At least that's what he looked like, his short brown and black fur was also greasy and matted, but he seemed in the best condition of the trio. At that moment the three dogs were little more than an irrelevant part of the scenery. But by dawn the next day I would come to respect the abandoned German Shepherd enough to name him Saint Jimmy, and the following is the tale of how that came about.

It was gone two in the morning, and I wanted to be at the bus depot for six just in case my guidebook was right and there was an earlier coach (or some other way to get to Antofagasta in time). I decided that it wasn't worth finding a hostel to stay in. Even if they did answer the door at that hour, I probably wouldn't be welcomed with open arms and I'd only have to leave a few hours later. All I needed was to find a secluded place to sleep in; a bench in a park perhaps. Tramps do it all the time, and Calama certainly seemed to have no shortage of them!

Getting up and shuffling along the street to find a suitable spot, I soon realised that I was being followed. My four-legged friends were with me as I walked down the street, but I presumed that they would soon get bored and leave me alone. However, I started to doubt this when after several blocks they were still with me. I began to try to purposefully lose them. I tried shouting, *stay! Stop!, Pare! And No!* In my best dog command voice, but none of it had any effect.

I began to break into short runs, but even when I managed to leave them behind, it took little time for them to magically reappear next to me again. By now I'd been going for over half a mile and was beginning to get desperate. I tried crossing a busy road, but the dogs always caught up, even when I was determined enough to cross back and forth several times, sometimes dangerously close to oncoming traffic! Eventually though I seemed to lose the large fluffy hound and the small 'handbag' one. But the young German Shepherd; St Jimmy, stuck with me relentlessly.

Night time in Calama appeared to be ruled by a massive tribal society of stray dogs. They were simply everywhere, like in a Disney film gone wrong. On every street corner and under every bench there were packs of them, outnumbering the humans by a large margin. I felt as if I'd slipped into a weird Sci-Fi world like the Planet of the Apes. But the armies of disgruntled monkey-men had been replaced with countless packs of filthy, barking hounds. I tried deliberately walking through groups of these to deter my pursuer. This sometimes worked as St Jimmy would often stop to sniff and or bark at them. Whenever this happened I took the opportunity to run away in an attempt to lose him. I would cross roads and change direction multiple times at various junctions.

One time I made it several blocks before I slowed down, checked that the coast was clear behind me, and breathed a sigh of relief that I had finally lost him. Then as I was trying to find my bearings and catch my breath, I took a look down, and 'pop' there he was, shiny eyes looking up at me as if I was his best friend!

Half-way through this charade, in one of the few moments when I thought I'd made good my escape, I chanced upon a large, modern-looking public building. It was quite well lit and looked like some sort of art gallery, theatre, or maybe community centre. What interested me at the time, was that it was surrounded by a public space filed with small trees, shrubs and simple concrete sculptures. This area was shielded from the road by a concrete embankment, atop which was a thin layer of earth that gave root to a few small, straggly, bushes.

Built into the side of the embankment and facing away from the road, were numerous semi-circular alcoves, each of which contained a thin palm type tree and a low stone bench. During the day it was probably the sort of place that people might relax with friends, or perhaps just sit and rest a while as the town bustled on around them. But at gone three o'clock in the morning on that miserable summer night, I decided that it was the nearest that I was going to find to a free, open-air, one-star hotel.

Laying down on a bench and using my pack as a pillow, I hoped to get three or four hours sleep before heading off once again to the bus station. But soon after

I had settled down in my temporary, open-roofed home, a skinny white dog that may once have been a poodle, jumped up onto the top of the embankment and stared aggressively down at me. Barely a second passed before it started to yapp away for all its worth. After all the effort that I'd put in that night (I was by this point, shattered), I thought that I'd just ignore the one territorial mutt and hope that eventually he would get bored and go away.

It was not long however before a woolly head rose above the parapet. The head was attached to a bulky canine body that sprouted a thick coat of fluffy brown and white hair. He added a deep throaty bark to the poodle's yapping, and was soon joined by another, and then another. In ones, twos and threes, dogs wandered over from all around and joined the group to play their part in the cacophony of noise. Before long they were arrayed everywhere. There must be twenty to thirty of them standing on the embankment above, and on the benches, sculptures and vegetation to my front. I had never seen such a varied collection of dogs all in the same place!

Big and small, fat and thin, cute and ugly, it seemed as though every breed was represented. Whatever their differences, at that moment they were all united in the cause of singing a chorus of discontent at the unwelcome intruder in their territory. On my earlier trek around the city, I'd thought it strange that the human tramps slept in the dingiest of shop doorways. Now I knew why; it was the dogs, not men, who were the kings of the streets here!

There was clearly no way that I'd be able to stay there. Even if I could somehow put up with the dogs, it wouldn't be long before the noise attracted unwelcome human attention. So yet again I wearily shouldered my heavy pack, and began to walk the streets once more. It wasn't long before St Jimmy appeared by my side again.

The only other hope I had of finding shelter that night, was at an area of deserted wasteland near to the outskirts of the city. I stared out into the darkness, trying to determine if the wasteland would be a safe place to lie up. But out of the silence of the night came yet more howls of numerous packs of dogs. Dejected and exhausted, I took the only option that I could then think of, and returned back to the bus depot from whence I began. It was on the way there that I decided to give St Jimmy his name. I had still given him no food, attention, or tried to befriend him in any way whatsoever. Yet for a reason that I couldn't possibly fathom, he had stuck by me for hours and miles; a greasy guardian angel in that city of dusty depression.

On my way up to the North I had spent the whole of Christmas Day in the departure lounge of Santiago Airport, waiting for my flight onwards. To occupy this time I spent some of my meagre funds on a cheap CD player, but only had enough money left over to buy one CD. After browsing for some time in the English language section of the airport's small store, I chose the album 'American Idiot' by the band Green Day. I proceeded to listen to this over and over again for the following four to five hours, and then many more times whilst on the coach to San Pedro. Among the many catchy songs was one entitled 'St Jimmy', and for no other reason than that the name seemed to fit, I had decided to christen my faithful German Shepherd companion with it.

Surely enough when I arrived back at the bus depot (for the third time that night), Fluffy and handbag were already waiting for me. I slumped on the perimeter wall and put on my hat, gloves and extra jumper for warmth. Despite being in the desert, it was very cold in those early hours. I put my large pack beneath my head, and the smaller one under my feet so that I would wake if any thieves were to try and take them in the night. As I lay there trying to get to sleep, Fluffy, Handbag and St Jimmy began to huddle closer. Still wary of their dirty state, I'd give them a firm, but not particularly hard, kick if they tried to get too close. Soon they too settled down to sleep in a huddle by my side, about a foot away from my comatose body.

Had St Jimmy known all along that I was destined to return to that spot? Or did he feel some sense of fellowship with me, another stray, alone and far from home? The answer I will never know. I'm certainly not a dog expert, and in truth I've no idea if he even was a German Shepherd. But I certainly welcomed the camaraderie and protection that he offered, without want of reward or recompense.

Drifting in and out of sleep, I could hear the whole city alive with the sound of dogs. But my companions

383

were blissfully silent. Several times in the night Fluffy and St Jimmy would suddenly start growling angrily and territorially, prompting me to open my eyelid just a slither to see what was going on. On each occasion the growling was directed at passers-by, people who, whatever their business at that time of night, were being warned off by my trio of ever vigilant protectors.

Upon waking shortly after sunrise, I decided that my friends deserved reward for their companionship. I took both packets of biscuits from my pack and emptied them out for them to feast on, making sure that Handbag also got her fair share. I would have expected the dogs to fight for the food, or wolf it down as quickly as possible, but instead they just steadily munched away, sharing the bounty out between them.

Making the most of the distraction, I went inside the bus depot, praying that there would be some extra coach to Antofagasta's airport that no one had known about the night before. But whoever my prayer was aimed at obviously wasn't listening, because nothing had changed from the previous night. The first coach was still not until 09:30, and I was still going to miss the flight. But then, just as panic was again starting to set in,

I looked up at the destination board and saw the word Santiago.

Of course! I was in Chile, land of excellent and cheap transportation. For £28 I could travel the entire 1,400 kilometres by coach! The trip would be a long one at twenty-two hours, but I needed some sleep anyway, and would still make it to Santiago with a few hours to spare before my flight to England.

The coach pulled out of Calama and headed south, carrying me away from the city of St Jimmy forever. The following twenty-two hours were mostly spent sleeping, with the occasional fifteen-minute break to stretch my legs when we stopped at some of the larger cities in Chile's northern half. At the journey's end the coach pulled into one of Santiago's major bus terminals, which at the time was a hive of activity. It bustled with all sorts of people from businessmen, to families off to visit relatives. Feeling dirty, woozy and disorientated, I stepped from the coach and made my way around to the side to collect my bags.

On the way, I almost walked straight into a small Chilean man in a dishevelled-looking brown leather jacket. We made slight eye contact and he motioned for me to go first. It was a strange gesture in the anti-social environment of a busy Santiago bus terminal. Nevertheless, I stepped forwards and waited for a space to clear in the disorganised rabble of people so that I might retrieve my bags from the bottom of the bus. Whilst waiting I must have felt the vaguest of sensations around the region of my left trouser pocket; the one in which I usually carried my wallet.

Without any conscious thought, I slapped my arm rapidly downwards, and to my great surprise come into contact with somebody else's hand! As I spun round I caught sight of the man who had let me pass moments before, now running hell for leather into the crowd. I did think for a moment about giving chase. But even in the unlikely event that I did catch him, how would I explain the situation to the authorities in a succinct manner without spending ages in a police station? My flight out of the country would be leaving in just a few hours, and after everything that I'd been through, I didn't want anything to get in the way of me making it.

So, I let him go, thankful that I was one of the very few people that had managed to foil one of these masters of their trade, and to have prevented the theft of my wallet and passport. In fact, had he pushed in front of me like everyone else in the queue, I'm sure that I'd never have been the slightest bit alerted, and he would have gotten clean away with it.

I still do not know how he knew exactly which pocket my wallet was in. Pickpockets the world over can never be underestimated. They will always strike when you are at your weakest, and are highly skilled at what they do. Even a person aware to the threat, may often easily be caught out in a moment of distraction or fatigue. The thief only has to get lucky once, but a traveller needs to be aware all of the time.

After heading into a packed public toilet, I was able to make an attempt at washing and somewhat reorganise my things. I then trekked into the city centre and caught the transfer bus to the airport. After checking in I stood in line at passport control, behind a large Chilean man who was being checked through by a stern-faced immigration policewoman. I was more than a little taken aback when the Chilean turned around, and with a look of surprised glee spread across his face greeted me with the words:

"Hey Wanker!!!"

Yes, out of the tens of thousands of people who passed through Santiago International Airport every day, I had managed to unwittingly queue behind the one person that I knew; Peque Manquilef himself. Unfortunately, we were going to the UK on different flights, but it was nice that my Chile experience was to end with yet another bizarre coincidence. It is strange how the longest country in the world, with its sixteen million inhabitants, can sometimes seem rather small.

Enjoyed the book?

Then please feel free to leave me a review on Amazon, Goodreads or any other platform of your choice. Good reviews and shares on social media help me hugely as a small independent author.

References

1. El cristo mapuche se perdió en el mar, El Diario Austral de Valdivia - 23 May 2010
2. http://www.remember-chile.org.uk/inside/ai84eight.htm
3. Voyage of the Beagle – Charles Darwin - 1839
4. Between Extremes – John McCartney and Brian Keenan – 1999

Memoirs of a Crow Bag

Steely-eyed dealer of death, holder of 100 confirmed enemy kills, Sword of Honour recipient, and winner of the Royal Signals junior officer essay writing competition.

Captain Lord was none of these things.

This is the story of one man's inept attempts to survive in the British Army during its most intense period of conflict for 50 years. But this is not a Ramboesque tale of contacts, getting rounds down, or 'slotting' the enemies of the Her Majesty the Queen. Rather it describes the antics of a man who was renowned more for his actions in the mess bar than on the battlefield.

Follow Lord through the ardours of the country's most esteemed military academy, and onwards through Germany and into the war in Afghanistan. Learn of the fear, thrills and tragedies that are part of the life experiences of a 21st century Army officer at war.

Then acquaint yourself with being trapped in a blind gay dwarf maze, berated by angry prostitutes, shot at by a brigadier with a potato cannon, shaved by an elderly sex fiend, a Para cock and a big pair of Commando balls, a naked encounter with a goat, the Cult of the

Tabasco Balls and the two different types of duck walk...

Coming Soon.

Printed in Great Britain
by Amazon